814.542

240

The Collected Wit and Wisdom of

JAMIE BUCKINGHAM

THE TRUTH WILL SET YOU FREE

BUT FIRST IT WILL MAKE YOU MISERABLE

Creation House
Altamonte Springs, Florida

Creation House
Strang Communications Company
190 N. Westmonte Drive
Altamonte Springs, FL 32714
(407) 869-5005

Illustrations by J. Colle

Second Printing, May 1989
Third Printing, September 1989

Dedicated to:

My long-suffering wife, Jackie, who laughs at me when I can't laugh at myself,

My five children and ten grandchildren, who laugh with me because they think I'm funny,

And my nervous publisher, Stephen Strang, who consults his lawyer every month to make certain my non-laughing readers can't sue his socks off.

Contents

Foreword

Always Two Steps Behind Jamie

Jamie and I have spent a lot of years walking around the kingdom. But as long as I can remember, he's always been several steps ahead of me. That's the reason I agreed to write this foreword. For once, I want to be first.

No matter whether we are taking a walk down our front drive to the mailbox, making our way through a crowded convention hall, leaving church and crossing the parking lot to the car—I'm always at least two steps behind my "in-a-hurry husband."

When I first complained about this several years ago, Jamie quickly pointed out this was an accepted practice in the Orient. He reminded me of the dinner we had in a posh restaurant in Seoul, Korea, with famed pastor Yonggi Cho. When the meal was over, Pastor Cho headed for the door, his good wife ten steps behind. The only time he stopped was when he reached the door—waiting for his wife to catch up so she could open it for him.

Jamie's not like that. He's just preoccupied. And in a hurry. And besides, he walks faster than I.

Maybe I'm slow because of the kind of shoes I wear—shoes made for standing and sitting, definitely not for walking, and certainly not for the kind of walking I have to do to keep up with my husband.

But it's more than that. Jamie's legs are longer than mine. When we both walk at our natural pace, he simply goes faster, as a horse walks faster than a pony. To stay together, either he has to slow down—or I have to trot. And up to this time neither of us has been willing to adjust our gait.

So I walk behind.

Jamie is goal-oriented. By that I mean when we hit the sidewalk he doesn't like to stop. I like to look in shop windows. When we walk into a department store he heads immediately for the place he intends to go: underwear, automotive parts, light bulbs or shotgun shells.

Me, I love to linger. I always pause and look at the first thing I see when I come through the door—usually something flimsy and feminine, or something for the grandchildren. When I look up, my husband is five aisles away, striding militantly past all those beautiful lamps and bedspreads, his eyes fixed on the hardware shelf like a batter trying to stretch a long single into a double.

All the while I'm back at home plate, chatting with the umpire about uniform styles for next season.

The same is true when we take one of our "strolls" in the woods or down a deserted beach. Sure, there are many times when he walks beside me, holding my hand—but those are the times when he needs to talk from his heart. The rest of the time I stroll and he marches, or jogs. That means the best I can enjoy of my husband is his backside—which, now in the latter half of his fifth decade, is not necessarily the most attractive part of his anatomy.

This used to irritate me. In fact, there were times when I would drop behind on purpose, just to make him slow down and notice me.

One time on a long walk through the North Carolina woods, I waited until he had marched around the next bend in the trail, then I turned around and went back to the house. He showed up thirty minutes later, marveling at how I had gotten in front of him and beat him home. He never seemed to realize he had taken "our walk" by himself.

Poor thing, he always has his mind on other things.

The problem is intensified when we take a drive together. I've learned to keep pencil and paper handy, for he is constantly asking for a notebook to jot down ideas that come to him—usually while we're speeding along the highway or making our way through city traffic.

I can't tell you how many times I've held the steering wheel and guided us along an interstate highway while he has written down some budding idea. We've even done it on the way to church meetings on Sunday morning as he's revised his sermon, written down the words of a song or remembered something he wanted to tell someone.

I suggested it would be much easier if I drove and he wrote. But the idea of my being in the passenger seat somehow makes him feel he is in control—even if I'm the one with my hand on the wheel.

That's pretty much the story of our lives together. He's the head of the home, but he doesn't mind when I remind folks that I'm the neck that turns the head. Actually, I'm more than the neck. I'm also the backbone that keeps him standing, the heart that keeps him feeling and the hand that pulls his foot out of his mouth.

However, I have resigned myself to the fact that when I walk with Jamie I will always be about two steps behind. Although there have been times when I felt he had left me to make my own way through life, I now realize we have always been, in a real sense, together. He leads the way. I follow in his footsteps—picking up the things he drops, or kicks over.

Walking behind my husband is an ideal place. From here I give him little shoves—to encourage him when he hesitates doing what God has told him to do. From this perspective I am able to nudge him in the right direction when he is tempted to stray off the path.

Little nudges from behind, I have discovered, are far more effective than playing the role of the bossy wife who tries to change her husband's direction by nagging and complaining.

My place, behind my husband, is also a place of safety. Jamie is always "out front." That means he's like the first duck off the pond—he's the one they shoot at. Back here, in his shadow, I feel safe.

But for once, I'm stepping out in front to write this foreword. As wild as it seems, not everything Jamie says in this book is exaggerated. Most of it grew out of very real experiences. The people, too, are real. I know—I've lived with them just as he has. Even though some of this stuff has shown up in his Last Word column in *Charisma*, most of it is original—meaning he's never had the courage to write about it before now.

One of our friends, Brooks Watson, the one who opened up Jamie's head on the racquetball court—yes, he tells that story too—says it's more fun to read Jamie's stories than to be there in person. Maybe, but it's also been a wonderful life to live in person. I hope this book will not only make you laugh, but it will nudge you—as I nudge Jamie—a little bit closer to God.

Jackie Buckingham
Melbourne, Florida

Introduction

If God Is God, Then Life Is a Comedy

I think it was Garrison Keillor of Lake Wobegon, Minnesota, who said, "If you believe in the existence of a loving and merciful God, then life is a comedy."

Keillor was not talking about comedy as in joke. He meant comedy in the Shakespearean sense—as opposed to tragedy.

In tragedy, things turn out badly. In comedy, all's well that ends well.

Bottom line: If God is really in control, we might as well enjoy life—rather than take it so seriously.

That upsets a lot of Christians because they take not only life but also themselves pretty seriously.

Keillor, I read somewhere, emerged from a strict fundamentalist background. Fundamentalists don't laugh very much. As one wag said, "Most fundamentalists are no fun, all damn and very little mental." Keillor's "Prairie Home Companion" radio program, however, caused a lot of laughs. On long, dark, winter nights, when the snow was up to the eaves, folks in Minnesota and Wisconsin huddled around their radios and listened as Keillor talked about life the way it should be—fun.

Keillor spoofed Father Emil, pastor of Lake Wobegon's Our Lady of Perpetual Responsibility Church. He reminded his listeners of the old priest's annual sermon on birth control. His text: "If you didn't want to go to Minneapolis, why did you get on the train?"

15

He also spoofed his parents, God-fearing Plymouth Brethren, who "believed there was a verse in the Bible—they couldn't find it, but it was there, maybe in Leviticus somewhere—that forbade air conditioning."

Now a lot of folks don't think Keillor is funny. They don't believe in a God who laughs. Christianity, they say, should be taken seriously.

Well, of course it should. The problem is we take ourselves—and other Christians—seriously also. Too seriously.

Several years ago I decided I was going to write a book entitled *Charismatics, Pentecostals, Evangelicals, Fundamentalists, Protestants, Catholics and Others Who Take Themselves Too Seriously.*

My wife, Jackie, said I was heading for big trouble. "Why don't you wait and write that book just before you die?" she said.

"What do you mean?"

"I mean, regardless of how long you live afterwards, it will be your last book. You won't have any friends left."

Now you have to understand my wife. She thinks I stir people up on purpose. One Sunday morning after church I saw a group of people out on the lawn, their faces red, teeth gnashing, shouting at my wife. She was equally angry, shouting back at them. Finally the group stormed off in all directions. I came out from behind the bush where I was hiding and asked Jackie what was going on. She said they were angry over my sermon that morning. They felt I had poked fun at them.

I thanked her for defending me.

"I wasn't defending you," she shot back. "I was agreeing with them."

Every Christian should read James Thurber—at least half as much as they read the Bible (which means once or twice a year). I'm grateful to my father, who taught college English before moving to Florida to go into business, for introducing me to Thurber stories such as "The Secret Life of Walter Mitty" and "Things That Go Bump in the Night." I've called on them many times.

For instance, a long time ago I was editor of the now-defunct *Logos Journal* magazine. In fact, a lot of magazines I once edited have since defuncted. The charismatic movement was going through one of its semi-annual crises at the time. Everyone's cage was being rattled by something called the "discipleship movement." A lot of people were angry with each other. Pat Robertson had gone on television and equated Bible teachers Bob Mumford and Charles Simpson with occult leader Jim Jones, who had just led a bunch of folks to commit suicide by drinking poisoned Kool-Aid. A California-based organization known as the Full Gospel Business Men's Fellowship had officially banned anyone remotely connected with "shepherding" from speaking in their meetings. (In fact, they even banned me simply because I happened to live in the state of Florida, which the California people had heard was somewhere near Ft. Lauderdale where the "shepherds" all lived.) Kathryn Kuhlman, who had a wonderful healing ministry, was convinced the discipleship movement was a spreading epidemic that needed healing. She went on television and called Bible teacher Derek Prince a false prophet, which is something like being a spiritual Typhoid Mary. It was an interesting time in the kingdom.

Somehow I wound up as chairman of one of the "reconciliation committees" that popped up like toadstools in a barnyard after a rainy night. One of our more infamous meetings was held in a schoolhouse outside Minneapolis. After two days of hearing witnesses from both sides of the controversy (everybody who was anybody was there), an Episcopal priest, whom many called the father of the charismatic movement, got so angry he threw his Bible on the floor. Shouting that he was tired of listening to blasphemy, he stomped out of a door—slamming it behind him.

We all sat in stunned silence. This was one of our most respected leaders. Then we heard all this noise behind the door. It sounded like buckets being overturned on the floor and sticks pounding against the wall. Moments later the door opened. There stood the respected cleric, his red face contrasting sharply with his white turn-around collar. Unfamiliar with the building, it seems he had stormed into a broom closet and gotten tangled up with the buckets and mops and things.

I went back home after the meeting (we never did settle anything) and wrote a "James Thurber" column in *Logos Journal*—which guaranteed its defunctness. Thurber, I recalled, had once written a story entitled "The Day the Dam Broke." It started out with a man dashing through the little town shouting, "Run for your lives, the dam has burst!" The entire town fled in panic. Women with nursing children ran awkwardly down the street. A man leaped from his barber's chair, lather on his face and a blue-and-white striped apron still around his neck,

17

to join the panic-stricken mob heading for high ground. Houses and stores emptied in an every-man-for-himself stampede. Finally, panting and out of breath, one fat man collapsed alongside the road.

"Go on," he motioned to the people fleeing past him. "I'll just have to drown in the flood."

But as he sat there, trying to catch his breath, a thought came to him. "What dam? There isn't any dam within a hundred miles."

Eventually, Thurber said, everyone came to the same conclusion and returned sheepishly to their town. The interesting thing was they never mentioned the incident again. It was as though the panic never happened.

Well, I suggested in my editorial that a sane approach to the discipleship movement—or anything-other movement—would be for the leaders to get together, laugh at each other and at themselves, and wait it out. "This, too, will pass," I concluded.

That made everyone angry and they defuncted the magazine.

Of course the editorial I wrote entitled "The Whiffenpoofs" probably helped finish us off. That was the one where I likened the leaders of the shepherding movement to the Yale seniors who raised their beer mugs down at Morie's and sang: "We are poor little sheep who have gone astray: Baaa, Baaa, Baaa!"

"Tell me you didn't write it," Bob Mumford pleaded with me. But I had.

A few years later, right on course, the discipleship movement did dissolve. About that same time, Kathryn Kuhlman went to heaven and discovered a lot of folks were there because the shepherds had pointed the way. Pat Robertson resigned from television and ran for president—which was really funny. The Full Gospel Business Men's Fellowship sent an investigator to Florida and discovered that Ft. Lauderdale was actually populated by Jews and Canadians, not shepherds. In fact, they couldn't find a single member of the old discipleship movement. All the Bible teachers had moved to Alabama and California and left me to run Florida the way it should be run. Like the folks in Thurber's parable, everyone had sneaked back into town and was going about business as usual.

"What panic?" they asked.

When I was ten years old, my daddy took me to Washington, D.C., to visit our esteemed senators and congressmen. Other than remembering the big argument between my father and the bellhop in the hotel after my mother tipped him a nickel for carrying our heavy suitcases up three flights of stairs, the only thing that stuck in my young mind was meeting old Sen. Herman Talmadge from Georgia. The senator was standing in the Senate bathroom combing his shock of unruly hair and snapping his red suspenders when my daddy introduced me. Looking down, he said, "Son, there's only one thing in life worth remembering."

Awed, I asked, "What's that, sir?"

"This, too, will pass, son. Remember that: this, too, will pass."

He then gave a big laugh, snapped his suspenders and returned to making laws that didn't make any sense.

Some things are so serious they can only be addressed by laughing at them. I think Jesus probably had to bite His tongue to keep from laughing at the stuffy fundamentalists of His day. He agreed with Garrison Keillor. He saw life as a comedy—not a tragedy. Why? Because He knew God was in charge of everything.

Now if that's really the case, why get upset over a few heretics, a couple of TV preachers who can't keep their pants zipped or someone's diagnosis that the church's wagon is going to hell and you've been handcuffed to the axle?

Why not sit back, enjoy life and chuckle at the nay-sayers?

Blessed is the man who can laugh at himself. In fact, that's a lot better than having a heart attack or ulcers, or putting a bump on your husband's head with a nine-pound Bible.

"A happy heart," Solomon once wrote, "makes the face cheerful." Then he expanded on that by saying, "A cheerful look brings joy to the heart, and good news gives health to the bones." A chapter later he puts in a word to denominational committees by saying, "He who loves a quarrel loves sin...but a cheerful heart is good medicine."

In short: Hey, loosen up, folks—God's in charge.

Maybe it's the way I was raised. Back in the late '30s and early '40s our family would spend Sunday nights sitting around a big, old, round-topped radio that had a wire running from the antenna screw to the copper screen in my parents' upstairs bedroom window. At 7 p.m. we'd shush one another and tune the dial to pick up the great Sunday night radio comedies: Jack Benny, Red Skelton, Edgar Bergen (along with Charlie McCarthy and Mortimer Snerd), and somebody named Henry Aldrich.

19

You remember him, don't you? Every segment opened with his mother screaming at him: "HENREEEEE! HENRY ALDRICH!" Gosh, how that sounded like my mother. Every time it would come on, my older brother, Clay, would mimic her: "JAMIEEEEE! JAMIE BUCKING-HAM!" Then he'd add my mother's famous admonition: "WHATEVER YOU'RE DOING, STOP IT THIS SECOND!" People have been saying that to me ever since.

Those great old shows parodied life. Today bad housekeeping is grounds for divorce. Back then we laughed when Fibber McGee opened his famous closet and was buried by Mollie's junk which came tumbling out.

That was a generation ago. Now everyone seems mighty serious. Some of my friends think Jesus is going to return no later than December 31, 1999. That means they've got a lot of serious work to do if they're going to straighten everything out by then. When you're in charge of the world, you don't have much time to laugh.

A few of my friends are bent out of shape about all the new heresies which keep appearing like mold on the walls of the temple—not to mention the rash of films and TV shows profaning the name of God, the purity of Jesus and the mission of the church.

And it's hard to believe there are still pockets of people who gnash their teeth when you mention the gifts of the Holy Spirit.

That's the reason I've written this book. I also wrote it because I wanted to say a bunch of things that my stuffy magazine editors won't let go into my magazine column.

So if you want to live long, be rich, glorify God and have fun—remember this: Life is a comedy. Each day is a wonderful adventure, full of fun and laughter. Most important, remember this: The truth will set you free, but first it will make you miserable.

Jamie Buckingham
Melbourne, Florida

ONE

My Washing Machine Has a Demon

After years of theological debate, I finally discerned why our thirteen-year-old Ripmore washing machine has been losing my socks. It's possessed. I mean, possessed as in demons. In short, I am convinced we have a sock-gobbling demon in our washing machine.

Now every kingdom person knows that mere recognition of the fact that you have a demon is ninety percent of the deliverance process. Most folks would rather have cancer than have a demon. My Ripmore has that, too, but it's the sock-gobbler that really got my attention.

My wife disagrees. She comes from the theological school that says Christians (or washing machines owned by Christians) can't have demons. I, on the other hand, believe a washing machine can have anything it wants to have.

"If there really is a sock-gobbler," Jackie asked, "why does he eat

21

only one sock out of a pair? If one sock fills him, why doesn't he eat the spare sock his next meal?''

I had no answer. I only knew he was there. To prove it I went up to my dresser, opened my sock drawer and pulled out the seventeen unmatched socks that I've been saving—widowed victims of the sock-gobbler. And that's just today's count. Each month or so I take a census. Like our church in Florida, the widows seem to be increasing in number. In fact, looking out over our congregation Sunday after Sunday, it seems we're producing more widows than new babies, but maybe that's because the new babies are always in the nursery and widows seem to bunch together, like raisins stuck in the bottom of the box or socks in the back of my sock drawer. That's the reason I hate to throw away the singles. Every time I start to do it I think, ''Now if you were left without a mate, would you want someone to throw you away?'' And I think about the running dialogue on worthlessness I used to have with Jackie during her monthly three-day, nobody-loves-me period.

''The only reason anyone tolerates me is because I'm married to you. If you were to drop dead—people would forget I even exist.''

I kept reminding her I planned to live to be 100. Facts, however, never faze a woman during her monthly three-day, nobody-loves-me period. And that's the reason I can't ever bring myself to throw away any of those widowed socks which keep increasing after every wash. In fact, I've been thinking recently of putting my underwear in the same drawer with the knit shirts I can't wear any more since our Ripmore shrank them all to grandchild size and then of setting up an entire drawer for single socks. I mean, churches used to have widows' pews, and we have a singles' group that meets on Tuesday nights, so why not a separate drawer for my recently bereaved socks?

The real reason I keep my unmatched singles, however, is that I keep hoping their mates will somehow reappear. It never happens. Each month or so I take them out of the drawer and sadly line them up across the bed, looking vainly to see if I can match any of them with each other. I never can. Expensive racquetball socks, formal blacks, blues, greens, grays, fuzzies—all were favorites, but without mates they're useless.

So I gently stuff them into the back of my sock drawer and wonder if I should form a club: Socks Without Partners.

At first I thought it was Jackie's careless washing procedures.

"The reason my socks don't come out even is you don't put them in even!" I howled when my most expensive and favorite pair of socks became a single.

"Not so," she argued. "I gathered them two by two. Believe me, Noah didn't do a more complete job. I took two pairs from your shoes under the bed, a pair of wet ones out of your boots, a stiff pair from the ceiling of the closet where you had kicked them when you came in from racquetball, a mud-caked pair from under the front seat of your pickup, a moldy pair from under the dryer—"

"A-ha!" I screamed. "I bet the rest of the mates are under the washing machine." However, my search turned up nothing but a bucketful of lint, three green pennies, two rusty washers, a twelve-year-old skate key and a flea collar from our cat, Mrs. Robinson, who preferred to scratch rather than be in legalistic bondage.

"Inside this washer is a little trap door that pulls in one sock from each pair and holds them captive," I concluded. "Somewhere in this machine is a secret treasure chest of mismated socks."

Several years ago I was greatly embarrassed when I stepped off the plane in Washington, D.C., for a book editorial meeting and discovered I was wearing one blue sock and one gray one. I explained to my snickering friends that these were the only ones in my drawer when I got up that morning to catch the early flight.

A week later I received a package in the mail from my friend John Sherrill, who had been at the editorial meeting. It contained a little mesh nylon bag with a zipper across the top. "Put your socks in this before you put them in the machine," John wrote. "Then the sock-gobbler can't get at them." (John, you see, agrees that washing machines can have demons.)

But he misjudged. The sock-gobbler not only ate my socks, but it also ate the bag.

"The machine is possessed!" I screamed at Jackie.

"Oppressed," she said, trying to straighten out my theology, "not possessed. See, your maroon socks always come out perfectly."

She's right. I hate the maroon pair. The elastic is stretched out and they have a big crease across the top, so every time I put them on they rub a blister on the toe next to my big toe. They come out of the washer even when you don't put them in. In fact, I distinctly remember dropping them in the trash one night after my wife had gone to bed. The next evening I was in the den watching the news on television when Jackie came out of the utility room with an armload of clothes. I couldn't believe my eyes. On top of the stack were those ugly maroon socks. I knew then I was dealing with something more than trap doors. Oppressed, possessed—this was no time to get hung up on theological semantics. The machine had a demon and needed deliverance.

The next morning, after Jackie had gone to a Bible study, I went upstairs and pulled out my mismatched socks. I laid them on the bed. The only socks left in my drawer were some black fuzzy ones that had shrunk up until they looked like those little things golfers pull over the heads of their clubs, two pairs of racquetball socks with the tops stretched out so they looked like shopping bags and, of course, the maroon pair.

I went out the next day and bought ten pairs of new socks, all the same size and color. Then I stopped by the church office to see if someone with a deliverance ministry would come out to the house. The church secretary suggested I switch to a Maytag. She grew up in the Church of God and doesn't believe a washing machine can have a demon either, especially a born-again Ripmore with a sanctified lint-trap. She told me frankly that, if I wanted the demon out (assuming there could be a demon, of course), I would have to exorcise it myself.

I was reminded of the British statesman who, on his deathbed, was counseled by his priest to "renounce the devil."

"Sir," the dignified old sinner answered, "when you're in my position you can't afford to agitate anyone."

I decided to leave the Ripmore alone—it just might start in on my underwear. Since Sears doesn't make the kind I like any more, I can ill afford to lose any underwear.

Not long ago Ann Landers wrote about sock-gobblers. Nearly 8,000 readers wrote back saying they had the same problems. One fellow from Nyack, New York, wrote that the socks die and are reincarnated as wire coat hangers. If you don't believe it, just go look in your closet.

Another said it had bothered him for years because he was sure his wife had a lover with one leg. He finally determined it was UFOs with magnets that drew his socks into outer space. No one, so far, has been able to disprove his theory.

A woman from Billings, Montana, said she called the repairman and he found twenty socks wrapped around the motor of her Ripmore—a discovery which saved her sanity since she felt for years she had been going slowly nuts.

When I got brave enough to expose the sock-gobbler in one of my magazine columns, people from all over the nation were set free. Most of those who wrote said that they had been in bondage for years to the false theology that washing machines can't have demons. Scores told me that, armed with the truth I had given them, they went boldly into their utility rooms and cast the demon out of the machine. Several said they distinctly heard it leave the machine and go down the drainpipe.

Not all were so spiritual, however. About half a dozen—humanists, no doubt—said it was simply a matter of the socks getting separated and being swept away in the spin cycle. Two of those, who I assume were Roman Catholics, said the missing socks were now abiding in sock purgatory in my backyard septic tank.

Three others sent me packages of little plastic rings that were made specifically to keep socks from being separated in the washing machine. You pull the toes of your socks through the little teeth inside the rings and drop them into your Ripmore. I tried it. The rings came off and got down inside the whirling mechanism of my machine. I was upstairs when it happened but heard the house beginning to vibrate. By the time I got downstairs to the utility room, the washing machine had come off its rubber feet and had clunked its way over to the fiberglass sink on the other side of the room, bashing all the plumbing out from under it. There was water everywhere. The washer was making a horrible noise and it smelled like burnt rubber. I was ashamed to tell the nice Ripmore repairman, who arrived nine days later, what had happened. But I did determine that the cure was worse than the disease—which is what I now call the sock-gobbling demon since my mother-in-law moved in. She's a Primitive Baptist who doesn't believe in demons at all. (It's far more respectable, I've discovered, to have a disease than it is to have a demon.)

Of course, the sock-gobbler hasn't touched the plastic rings. (Maybe it was because he couldn't chew them up.)

Many sympathetic people, hearing of my need, have written helpful notes advising me how to solve my problem. Some say I should pin my socks together, others say tie them together, and one woman said she always stuffs them into the pockets of her husband's pants. One woman from Hendersonville, North Carolina, even wrote a poem entitled "Oh, Where, Oh, Where Is the Other Sock?" (Sung—at least every other line or so—to the tune of "Oh, Where, Oh, Where Has My Little Dog Gone?")

> They're under the bed or caught in the casters,
> Or clinging to the basement rafters.
> Trapped in the plumbing, stuffed in a shoe;
> In darkened corners hiding from you.
> They've gone to the camp, returned alone,
> Been kicked off by the telephone.
> An argyle lined a starling's home,
> A striped sock found its way to Rome.
> Perhaps there is an "odd sock" elf,
> Who takes them to some woodsy shelf.
> But truthfully I know their fate,
> The dirty ones disintegrate.

I'm grateful for all the people who across the years have shown concern for me in my affliction. I am now convinced that Paul's mysterious "thorn in the flesh" was in actuality a sock-gobbling demon that accompanied him on all his missionary travels, causing him to be the laughingstock of churches throughout Asia Minor. It's embarrassing, you know, to show up for a catacomb meeting wearing one brown sock and one blue one. And when all your shoes are open sandals, there's no way to hide the fact that, while your preaching may be saintly, your washing machine is definitely possessed.

It is doubtless for this reason Paul began washing out his socks by hand. This was especially important after he arrived in Macedonia because the Greeks would never have submitted themselves for deliverance to a man who obviously could not exorcise the demons from his own washing machine. (Several renowned theologians interpret Acts 16:13, which in most Bibles reads, "On the Sabbath day we [Paul and Luke] went outside the city gate to the river, where we expected to find a place of prayer," more accurately to mean "where we expected to find a place to wash our socks.")

Recently I've decided to follow Paul's example, washing my socks out by hand and hanging them on the shower rod. However, our oldest son, who lives with us, wears socks the same size as mine. Each time he wears them they disappear completely. Not just one, but both of them—before they even get to the machine. Early in the morning he comes in and gets mine off the shower rod, stretches out the tops, tears holes in the toes and leaves them on the back porch stuffed into his shoes when he comes in from work.

Like the folks in my church in Florida, old socks never die; they just fade away.

TWO

Unsystematic Theology

Things That Go Squish in the Night

One of the advantages of living in the country is the quietness.

One of the disadvantages is having to fool with a Rube Goldberg water system which pumps water out of the ground from a deep well and into our house through a nightmarish network of pumps, pipes, valves, joints and tanks.

I used to complain, when we had our house in the subdivision, about the cost and taste of Florida water. But now, after having moved out into the country—and having become an expert on wells, pumps, aerators, pressure tanks, green sand filters, chlorinators and water softeners—I'm not so sure I wasn't better off when all I did was turn on the faucet, hold my nose and pay the bill.

29

Our particular system works from a deep artesian well. The same well serves the house, sprinkling system and air-conditioning/heating units. After flowing through all the contraptions inside a little pump house in the backyard, the water usually arrives where we live. The majority of this water is drunk, flushed, spilled or used for washing. The rest is piped through the heating units and out through a drainpipe into a pond in the pasture.

To give the system a certain romance, the mad plumber installed a number of secret valves. If these are not opened and closed at critical times and in a particular sequence the water overflows into the yard, backs up into the bathrooms and floods the house, causes things in the pump house to explode (as they do at least every other year), or other exciting things.

One of these secret valves is connected to the drainpipe going from the air-conditioning/heating units in our house to the pond. It is located in the backyard at the edge of the pasture, tucked under the barbed wire fence which has recently been electrified in hopes of restraining my son's two wild cows with long, sharp horns. In case I want to divert this ever-running stream and use it to wash the car, I only have to turn the valve and open a spigot.

There is one major problem. The cutoff valve which diverts the water from pond to spigot is located in a concrete block which is buried about eighteen inches in the ground. To turn the valve, you have to lie down on your stomach and stick your hand down that dark hole.

The other night, after having told my teenage daughter to get her shower and go to bed "or else," a term both of us know is meaningless, I went to bed. Jackie was already asleep when I heard this strange gurgling in the heating unit at the end of the hall. I suddenly remembered I had forgotten to reopen the valve after I washed the car that afternoon. That meant the water was either about to overflow out of the heating units into the house or it already was flooding the backyard— or the pump house was getting ready to explode again. I leaped from bed, grabbed my flashlight and raced down the stairs and out the back door.

The backyard was flooded, and there was a strange high whine that was coming from the pump house and growing in intensity. Sloshing through the icy water in my bare feet, getting my pajamas wet up to my knees, I dashed to the pump house where I cut off all water to the house. This took care of the high whine but at the same time revealed a much deeper rumbling in the pressure tank connected to the water softener. Something horrible was getting ready to happen.

Cold, wet and barefooted, I gingerly headed out across the pitch-black yard, feeling my way between the pines and palmetto patches, to the edge of the pasture where the monstrous cows with the sharp horns lived. I had to locate that underground valve.

Kneeling in the cold mud beside the sunken valve, I foolishly forgot to look down the hole with my flashlight before putting my hand in there. When I put my hand in the hole I felt something move. Something slimy.

I withdrew my hand at great speed and at the same time leaped high off the ground from my kneeling position. Unfortunately, I had forgotten I was directly beneath the electrified barbed wire fence. The result was disastrous.

When I became a Christian, I lost most of my old vocabulary. This robs me of the necessary safety valve to handle such emergencies. So instead of cursing, I threw my flashlight at one of the cows who was standing there laughing at me. That not only left me in total darkness, but now I heard snorting and pawing in the darkness.

Ripping myself loose from the barbed wire, which had been sending electric shocks through my body every 1.3 seconds, I staggered backwards away from the fence and the snorting sound. In the process, I stepped in a huge pile of doggie-do. Suddenly I remembered one of those long-forgotten words and was just about to utter it, hoping my wife—who even though she was still sleeping was surely to blame for all this—would hear and repent. Just at that moment, hopping around in the high grass, I ran a thorny briar between my big toe and the toe right next to it—in a place where nothing harsher than a washcloth had been in forty years.

Suddenly the entire vocabulary returned, complete with expletives I never even dreamed of as a youth. This time I woke up not only my guilty wife but my neighbors on both sides of the property who lived a quarter mile away. Lights were flashing on all over the place as I went crashing back through the shrubs toward the house, my pajamas ripped half off, my back and neck and toe bleeding profusely. This time

I would blame not only my wife but also my daughter, my son who was away at college (this was certainly worthy of a long-distance phone call), and our sleeping dog who never moves from his place across the door sill where he sleeps day and night in order to trip burglars when they try to enter.

I had stopped to wash the doggie stuff off my foot in the flooded backyard when I heard my daughter shouting from upstairs, "Hey, I'm all soaped up, and there's no water in the shower."

Although I was back in control with the choice of words, I didn't seem able to control the volume. Thus I informed her, with a roar that was surely heard a mile away, that there was plenty of water down where I was and if she was unhappy she ought to join me.

Jackie finally came down the stairs in her bathrobe, and between us we got the valve shut and the water turned back on. We never did find out what that slithery thing was in the hole.

The television preacher, the night before, had told me God wanted me to be successful. What he didn't tell me was that the ladder to success is strung with barbed wire. Jackie gently reminded me that God is more interested in what I become as I climb the ladder than whether I ever reach the top. I suspect, by the way, the top is growing taller the more I climb, anyway.

So I'm out a brand new three-battery flashlight. (That pawing I heard was the cow putting my flashlight out of its misery.) I'm also out a perfectly good pair of pajamas and I can't wear my left shoe for a week since my foot is all bandaged up. Not only that, my children have drawn up a huge poster and stuck it above the bathtub with arrows that point to off and on, hot and cold, and a warning not to stick my hand down the drain.

Fortunately, no one else knows. You see, we live in the country where things are quiet.

Acts of God

I picked up the paper this morning and read where another sinkhole opened up and swallowed a heathen's house in Orlando. It started my day off right just to know that God was in charge and still showing folks that He's keeping His eye on sinners and saints alike.

Down here in Florida we have an interesting underground geological formation which causes these sinkholes.

During the dry season, some of the cells in the giant honeycomb strata beneath our state—which are ordinarily filled with water—often go dry. When that happens the earth above settles. Rapidly.

Yesterday in the Orlando suburb of Winter Park, the earth opened up and swallowed a house, a business and several expensive cars. All in a few hours.

Immediately a lot of us checked our insurance policies. Even though the house that fell into this last sinkhole was owned by heathens, I sort of suspected that, if the rain falls on the just and the unjust, it could be possible that the just might get caught in a sinkhole, too. That was when I discovered that most policies written in Florida have a special clause in the fine print called the "sinkhole exclusion" clause.

Sinkholes, say the insurance companies, are "acts of God" and cannot be covered.

Other "acts of God"—things which are not likely to happen, such as hurricanes, tornadoes, even lightning strikes—are covered. But sinkholes, which are more and more likely as we waste our rapidly diminishing water supply, are excluded.

Actually, sinkholes are not acts of God. They are really acts of man. When government agencies such as the U.S. Army Corps of Engineers dig huge canals to drain the swamps, when land developers dig thousands of deep wells to pump the underground water to the surface, the water table drops lower and lower and eventually something caves in.

Now if you're a heathen and you've just built your new home on top of the cave-in or just parked your expensive Porsche over the sinkhole, and you go rushing down to your insurance company, you'll be told with a sad smile that what just happened was an act of God and is not covered.

That's really unfortunate, for it causes heathens to blame God for something caused by the Army Corps of Engineers. Now if you're a Christian and the insurance company tells you a sinkhole is an act of God, you can stand up for your rights. After all, you're supposed to know more about God and His acts than any insurance company—even the big ones, who probably hire theologians to determine which are acts of God and which are not. But if you're a simple heathen and your only knowledge of God comes from some suspender-snapping, toupee-flopping television evangelist, you're at a real disadvantage when it comes to arguing with the insurance companies.

In case you're wondering what an "act of God" is and you can't find it in your concordance, you can sometimes find the definition in the tiny type on the back side of page thirteen of your insurance policy.

One definition reads something like this: "Any event, act or circumstance...whose occurrence could NOT be prevented by man."

That takes in things like seas which open up for Jews and close down on Egyptians, and suns which stand still when God's army needs a few more hours of daylight to whip up on the combined armies of the Amorites. It also includes things like demons fleeing before the man who speaks in the name of Jesus, and sick people whom doctors call terminal being healed when godly folks pray for them. Now those are real acts of God—but you never find that kind of thing in the fine print of your insurance policy. No, all you find is stuff like sinkholes and other disasters.

You can argue until you're blue in the face that sinkholes are actually the responsibility of the Corps of Engineers or your local developer, but it's all to no avail. Sinkholes are legally, on no less authority than the state insurance commissioner, an act of God.

According to the legal description, acts of God are: one, rare; two, undesirable; and, three, things to be prevented if possible. In short, acts of God, according to the insurance people, are things we would prefer not to happen and would prevent if we could.

It wasn't until I got concerned about sinkholes that I began to understand why so many Christians are afraid of the supernatural, the mystical, the charismatic aspect of our faith. We have been conditioned to believe that any act of God which has not been voted on, budgeted for and approved by the long-range planning committee—and which is likely to startle us or interrupt our life-style—is to be avoided at all cost.

Someone once told me about a little boy whose mother tucked him into bed, turned out the light and went down the hall to her room to read. In a few minutes, the little boy, dragging his teddy bear, was at his mother's door.

"Mommy, it's dark in my room. I'm afraid."

"Don't be scared, son," she said reassuringly. "God is in your room.

Go back to bed.''

The little kid trudged back down the hall and stood at the door of his bedroom. Peering into the darkness, he finally got up enough nerve to stick his head into the room.

"God?" he whispered.

No answer.

"God," he said again more boldly, "if You're in there, don't move! You'll scare me to death."

Most heathens, I've discovered, expect God to act. Those in the Far East are constantly leaving food in their spirit houses, consulting the shamans, trying to appease the volcanoes. Back in the States the average guy at the ballgame or in the bar, even though he never sticks his head in the door of a church, is still aware God is a God of action.

But when it comes to the average church member, well, we want God all figured out. We want to organize Him, tell Him when He can move and when He can't, and then we do everything we can to prevent Him from acting—especially if it might inconvenience us.

Deep inside, Christians know acts of God are not limited to volcano eruptions, tidal waves or sinkholes. We know God acts personally. He invades our lives, gives direction, chastises us when we need correcting, and blesses us simply because He loves us. We sense in our deepest spirit that He will act to conform us to the image of His Son if we only cooperate, that He will heal our bodies if we submit to His touch, that He will use us in a mighty way if we yield to Him.

But that's where we falter. We're afraid He might scare us. He might ask us to change. He might uproot us and send us to Africa or, even worse, tell us to start tithing our income to our local church.

So we invent elaborate schemes in our lives and our churches to prevent God from acting. And we add clauses to our church policies to make sure we're not held responsible in case He does act.

Several years ago I attended a church conference in the Rocky Mountains of Colorado. During the afternoon session the woman leader was conducting one of those little "imagination exercises." She stood on the platform speaking softly to the congregation.

"Imagine you are in a quiet garden. You are walking down a grassy path beside a bubbling brook. Birds are chirping. Now Jesus appears beside you. He has something to say to you. Listen."

She paused. We were all supposed to listen while Jesus spoke in the garden. Suddenly, in the quiet, an old man in the back of the auditorium began to speak in a cracked, quivering voice.

"I, the Lord, have something to say to you—"

The woman leader immediately interrupted. "Sir! Sir! Please sit down. Be quiet. You're disrupting the service."

The old man continued to prophesy. "I am not pleased with your programs and sacrifices. I desire—"

There was a hurried and embarrassed conference on the platform as the woman leader whispered desperately to two men behind her. "Who is that old man? What's he doing? Someone has to stop this."

At the leader's direction, two ushers gently took the old man by the arms and convinced him to sit down and be quiet.

After the meeting I made my way to the back of the auditorium. Something was bothering me about the way the thing had been handled and I wanted to meet the old fellow. When I spoke to him I discovered he was quite deaf. He couldn't hear a thing. I finally had to talk to his middle-aged daughter who was with him. She was weeping over what had taken place.

"Dad can't hear a word," she said. "He's been deaf for years. But he's never done anything like this—I mean, speaking out in a meeting. He was sitting here snoozing when the lady on the platform said that God wanted to speak to us. Suddenly his head snapped up and before I knew it he was speaking, saying God had something He wanted us to hear."

Unfortunately, there was no place in the order of service for God to speak—much less act—so we just missed out.

So we shuffle on, writing our own exclusion clauses, relegating acts of God to volcanoes and sinkholes. And we wonder why we never seem to hear—really hear—what God is saying.

Thank God for Extremists

If the "renewal movement" hasn't done anything else, it has at least reinstituted the office of the extremist in the church.

There is a difference between an extremist and a fanatic. A fanatic is someone who has lost his way and redoubled his effort. He makes up for his spiritual emptiness with noise and activity. He is as dangerous as he is insensitive. Get close to one and, like the drowning man in the lake, he's liable to pull you under with him.

I remember years ago quoting Vance Havner to Adrian Rogers, who was later elected president of the Southern Baptist Convention. It was Havner who said he'd rather try to restrain a fanatic than resurrect a corpse.

"Maybe so," Rogers quipped in reply, "but at least a corpse won't stab you in the back."

He's right. Fanatics are dangerous, especially when they occupy a high office and are backed by Bible-waving militants shouting, "Inerrant!" In some sectors this is the Christian equivalent of "Jihad!"— the Arab word for Holy War.

The extremist, though, is a different breed. He is full of life and knows where he is going. The problem comes when he gets so far out in front of everyone else that we lose sight of him, or he gets eaten by a bear. Even so, he is alive and kicking—although his foot may sometimes be in your ribs (or his mouth). But that's a whole lot better than being stone-cold dead in the market like a lot of cultural Christians.

I'm not afraid of extremists. Like Havner, I'd much rather try to restrain one than resurrect a corpse.

A friend and his wife recently returned from a harrowing vacation in Western Canada. On a lonely road high in the mountains they parked their car and started to climb down a steep hill toward a small stream far below, where they intended to eat their picnic lunch.

Halfway down the steep, rocky hill the wife slipped. Screaming in terror, she fell headlong over a cliff and landed at the bottom of the ravine. When the frantic husband reached her, she was lying face down in the stream, seemingly lifeless. The water around her was slowly turning pink from a nasty cut on her head.

Her husband was panic-stricken. Pulling her from the icy water, he laid her body on the bank and applied mouth-to-mouth resuscitation. There was no response as he blew into her mouth time and time again.

He pumped her chest. Then he blew some more. More pumping. More blowing. No response.

Finally, in desperation, he cried out to God. Loudly. Then he bent over, put his mouth against hers and blew again.

She came alive. And bit off the end of his tongue when her jaws snapped shut.

Last week, when I heard him testify of the miracle, he was the happiest man I'd ever heard. Even if he did talk with a decided lisp.

Life, even if it kicks and bites, is better than no life at all.

I love the extremist.

Every genuine Christian movement in history has begun with extremism. When a clock pendulum has hung motionless for a long time, it takes a big push to get it started. A little nudge won't do it. Even if the pendulum is only supposed to move in a four-inch arc, it will take a twelve-inch push to get it started.

The problem arises when some fanatic comes along and thinks he has to keep pushing the pendulum. These pushers (often disciples of the original extremist who got the pendulum swinging in the beginning) seem to think if big arcs are good, bigger arcs are better. They are unable to realize the clock needs to tick at its own pace, not in syncopation with their hyperactivity.

Equally bad is the frightened person who sees a corpse come to life and panics—desperately trying to shove it back under the ground. Such pendulum-stoppers use stereotyped phrases:

"Remember Aunt Emma who spoke in tongues and wound up in the insane asylum...."

"The next thing those cell groups will do is swap wives."

I believe the Holy Spirit is responsible for some of the extreme movements today. Granted, it seems the old clock is about to jump off the mantle rather than keep time as it should. But if the rest of us can hold steady while the pendulum finds its arc, we'll be back in motion again.

God always chooses the extremists to get us going, however.

Those early disciples were extremists. So was Luther. And John Hus. And Latimer and Ridley. When John Knox began talking about covenant relationship, it led to a civil war. And what about St. Francis, who took off his clothes?

I keep thinking about those thirty-one Anglican bishops who gathered in Canterbury Cathedral back in 1978. Led by Bill Burnett, the archbishop of Capetown, they danced around the high altar following holy communion. Bishops and archbishops dancing around the high altar? It started when one of the men gave a prophecy that some in the cathedral that evening would be martyred for their faith. They got so excited about being martyred that they danced. That sounds pretty extreme to me.

So this latest movement has spawned—or been spawned by—our own extremists.

Remember those deliverance services when everyone was handed a whoopee bag and told to vomit up their demons on the count of three?

And all that "falling under the power" with some evangelists even keeping a body count of how many went down in their meetings?

Then it was discipleship.

And all that talk about community.

Some of us even got involved in buying and storing emergency rations, preparing for the "tough times" which were just around the corner. I still have a year's supply of nitrogen-packed soybeans—with a shelf-life of sixteen years—stored under my bed in case tough times arrive during the next sixteen years. (Sigh!)

Yet someone has to set the pendulum in motion.

The kingdom clock, it seems, has been resting at five minutes after nine o'clock in the morning ever since 1960. How easy it is to taste life and then settle back in comfort—forgetting the spring needs to be wound on a daily basis. So every year or so a new extremist appears on the horizon shouting, "Follow me, boys!" Fortunately, he's usually moving so fast very few of us can keep up. But the thundering herd around us forces us along, and before we know it, we're back in motion.

Thank God for extremists. Every movement needs one.

But only one, thank you. Only one!

Who Turned Up the Pressure?

Most of the things I fix are fixed almost perfectly.

When I fix the drain under the sink, it almost stops leaking.

When I work on my car, it almost starts.

When I tell my wife I'm sorry, she almost believes me.

A lot of folks are that way with their spiritual life. They almost don't sin, and when they do it's just a little, and God knows they almost didn't.

Most of us are able to cover up our messes—almost. And we can usually get away with it—for a while. That is, until a crisis comes along or someone turns up the pressure. Then it's Katie-bar-the-door.

Like the time I decided to install an underground sprinkling system in my yard. Contrary to California propaganda, it does not rain all the time in Florida. In fact, there are times when we go for hours without rain. Even so, in order to maintain status in the neighborhood, I decided I needed a sprinkling system.

"You'll also need a plumber," Jackie said. "Remember the time you decided to fix the drain under the sink and it wound up costing you more than a new sink?"

"That was because the threads on the pipes were corroded. Could I help it if the sledgehammer slipped and broke the garbage disposal unit and shorted out the dishwasher?"

"The plumber said you should have stuck to preaching," she said wisely. "He said only a preacher would have tried to fix a loose pipe with a sledgehammer. This time, please call a plumber before you go messing around with the water system."

Plumbers are hard to find in our town, however. Most of them only work two days a week and then you have to make a reservation, like you do for a tee time at the golf course or a seat on an airliner. Besides, they all have busy schedules—racing sports cars and flying off to Acapulco.

I probably wouldn't have thought of how much I needed a sprinkling system except a friend gave me his old one. He had just installed a new system, complete with pop-up heads and an automatic time sequence. Since he hated to throw away all the old pipes and sprinkler heads, he dropped them by my house.

"At least missionaries get old clothes," Jackie said sadly. "But you... you get a hand-me-down, broken-down sprinkling system."

"Look at it this way," I said optimistically. "It's free."

"The Bible says, 'Every good and perfect gift is from above,' " Jackie intoned, quoting an old Sunday school memory verse. "There's nothing good and nothing perfect about this gift. That means it's not from above, it's from below—from the pit." She spelled it out as she always does when she wants to emphasize something: "P-I-T!"

"Just look at it," she said, pointing to the piles of old PVC pipe lying in the front yard. "Your 'friend' had to dig it out of the P-I-T!"

"But he's an influential member of the church. I'd insult him if I didn't install it."

Jackie's eyes take on a strange look when I use arguments like that. "The reason he gave it to you is you've been insulting him for years—ever since he started wearing that toupee. I told you, if you kept making fun of men who buy their hair rather than grow it, one of those rug-wearers would find a way to get even. This one has."

There's no sense in arguing with a a stubborn woman—especially when she's right. I knew I could install the thing *almost* perfectly. Since it never occurred to me to call my across-the-street neighbor who is in the landscaping business and has a big sign on the side of his truck that says "Underground Sprinkling Systems Installed," I decided to do it myself.

With the help of my children, I managed to dig up the yard and lay what seemed to be endless miles of PVC pipe. Then, using an abundance of tape, glue and clamps, I got the thing hooked up. Like repairing a locomotive that is roaring down the tracks, the job was technically interesting but not much fun.

Another friend gave me a rebuilt one-half-horsepower pump which I hooked to a pipe that ran into the lake in our backyard. Presto, we had water on the lawn.

Almost.

Something was wrong. It wasn't so bad that the pump kept sucking fish and frogs into the system and depositing them—in little bitty pieces—all over the lawn, which caused a horrible smell and brought my Jewish neighbor over one afternoon to inquire if God was visiting our neighborhood with the plagues of Egypt. A simple screen over the end of the pipe took care of that. The bigger problem had to do with water distribution. Unless we had a strong east wind, a portion of the yard never got wet. Besides, the pump kept breaking down.

After months of fiddling with the thing—installing new sprinkler heads, digging up the pipes and re-locating them—I finally determined the system was like my spiritual life: it needed more power.

"That tiny pump just isn't doing the job," I told Jackie. "I'm going to go down and buy a brand new two-horsepower baby. That'll take care of everything."

"Won't a huge pump like that cause a lot of problems?" Jackie said, looking at me sideways out of the corner of her eye.

"All it needs is more power. After all, I put it together myself."

"That's what I'm afraid of. Before you spend all that money why don't you—?"

But I was already out the door and on the way to the pump store. One thing I've learned in life: it doesn't do any good to argue with my wife when it comes to things I know more about than she does. What I needed from her was what every man needs from his wife—support and encouragement, not all those questions. Besides, the thing was almost working.

I spent most of a Monday running a larger intake pipe out into the lake and installing the new pump. Then came the moment of truth as I stepped over to the post where the switchbox was located.

"Don't you think it would be a good idea to tape up all those exposed wires before you turn it on?" Jackie asked.

"I just want to check it out," I assured her. "I'll tape them up after I see if it works."

"Honey, I wish you—"

But I knew what I was doing and flipped the switch. The pump whirred into life and we had water.

I mean, we really had water.

Where my old system—held together with glue, rotting tape and rusty clamps—had been sufficient for the little pump, something really exciting happened when it was connected to the big, new two-horsepower pump.

Water squirted everywhere. Underground connections burst loose and erupted in the yard like geysers, blowing dirt and grass all the way up onto the roof of the house. Tape peeled off exposed connections, sending out streams of water. Tiny pinholes in the pipes, unnoticed before, suddenly opened to spray water in all directions. Loose sprinkler heads were blown high into the air as water roared upward in gushers. Flaws, blemishes and defects which had remained undetected were immediately exposed as the new power surged through the system.

"It looks like you, after you received the baptism in the Holy Spirit," Jackie said, standing in the doorway holding an umbrella. "You thought you were perfect until God turned the pressure up. Talk about leaks. You looked like a sieve."

I was in no mood for a theological debate. "I can't get the thing turned off," I shouted, pointing to the switchbox which was right over a huge geyser and was shooting sparks all over the place.

"That's what happens when you're filled with the Holy Spirit," Jackie said, going back in the house. "Shows up every flaw."

Suddenly, miraculously, the pump went off.

"Everything's OK," I shouted through the back door. "It shut off by itself."

"I know," Jackie said. "I threw the circuit breaker. I've also phoned across the street and asked our neighbor to come over and try to salvage this mess."

"But it's almost fixed," I moaned, knowing it was time to give in.

My neighbor showed up the next afternoon. He said if I wanted to stick with the new power he'd have to replace my old pipes. I told him I understood the principle and agreed to keep out of his way and leave my sledgehammer in the garage.

It's too bad, though. I almost had it working.

Auctioning Off the Family Treasure

Every family has some kind of family treasure. For some it may be a christening gown, passed down from generation to generation. For others it may be a silver service, a piece of jewelry or some other family heirloom.

Our family treasure was a five-dollar gold coin, minted shortly after the Civil War began. It had been passed on from my great-grandfather to my grandfather to my father. My daddy kept it in a little copper matchbox, wrapped in string, hidden in the back of a big safe in his office.

On occasion he would let me open the safe, take out the box, untie the string and peer at the shining gold coin nestled in the yellowed cotton. No one was allowed to touch it for fear of tarnish.

That gold piece survived more than a century of hardship. It stayed in the safe during the great gold recall of the Depression. When thieves broke through the roof of my father's office, they missed the gold coin in the copper matchbox. It was as if God Himself were protecting it—preserving it as He had the traditions of the church—so it could be passed along to future generations.

On my twenty-fifth birthday, in a little ceremony in our home, my father passed the family treasure along to me.

My dad gave a little speech, tracing the history of the gold coin back to the time it was minted. His grandfather, who had earlier fought with the Confederacy, was the first owner of the coin. It had been given to him—by General Ulysses S. Grant personally—when he defected from the South, avowing he could no longer fight on the side of slavery. "A man of principle," General Grant had called him.

"General Grant admonished my grandfather to keep the coin forever in the family," my father said, "as a symbol of men who are willing to turn their back on all that is precious in order to take a stand for that which is right."

With that, my father handed me the coin. "The Buckingham men are men of principle," my father said, with a catch in his voice. "May the genuine gold of this coin ever remind you—and your children and your children's children—of the grand tradition of purity and principle we live by."

Because of the family treasure, Jackie and I rented our first safe-deposit box. Anything that precious should not be lying around the house where thieves might break in and steal it.

Across the years I would take my children with me into the vault at the bank where we would look reverently at the little gold coin, nestled in the cotton of the old matchbox.

The year our oldest son, Bruce, turned twenty-five I decided it was time to release the family treasure into his hands. In a little ceremony at the house, I related how it had come down to us through hardship, trial and suffering. It was, so to speak, our link with the past. I repeated, word for word as I remembered it, how Great-Grandfather Buckingham, a twenty-five-year-old orphan, had laid down his heritage as well as his musket to take a stand for principle and freedom.

"The Buckingham men are men of principle," I told Bruce. "May the genuine gold of this coin ever remind you—and your children and your children's children—of the grand tradition of purity and principle we live by."

Then, in what seemed to be an almost sacred moment, I placed the gold coin in his hands.

There were some tears. Some rejoicing. The exchange had been made. The treasure was still in the family.

Shortly afterwards Bruce called me on the phone. He had read an article in a national magazine on rare coins. Our particular coin—at least one like it—was listed as having great value. According to the magazine, five-dollar gold coins like ours were worth $1,925 if they were in reasonable condition.

Reasonable? Our coin was just as it had come from the mint. It had never been touched except by gloved fingers. For a century and a quarter it had rested in that little copper matchbox, surrounded by cotton—protected by the blood of the Buckinghams. It had never spent a day in anyone's purse, much less rattling around some man's pocket with common coins.

It was the family treasure.

More practical than sentimental, Bruce pleaded for patriarchal permission at least to get an estimate on the coin while the price of gold was up.

"That coin has been handed down from generation to—"

"I know, Dad," Bruce interrupted. "I'm not going to sell it unless you approve. But wouldn't it be a good idea just to know exactly what it is worth?"

"The coin is yours, Bruce," I said sadly. "Like all traditions, it is only as good as the one in whose hands it rests. You must follow your conscience on this matter. Remembering the words of General Ulysses S. Grant...."

Bruce took off from work the next day to drive the seventy miles to Orlando where the state's finest rare coin expert had a shop. That evening he returned and stopped by our house.

"You better be seated when I tell you this," Bruce said.

I glanced at Jackie, braced for what was about to come and took a seat at the breakfast table.

"I had the coin appraised. Guess what? It's *counterfeit*."

"What? It can't be. It has been passed down from generation to generation. It's the family treasure."

"Sorry, Dad," Bruce said wistfully. "But in this case the family treasure is counterfeit. The coin expert said there were lots of counterfeit coins minted during the Civil War. They were used by the Yankees to entice Confederate soldiers to defect and join the Union. This is one of them."

"You mean, not only is the coin counterfeit, but Great-Grandfather

45

Buckingham was an Esau—a mercenary who sold his great Southern birthright for a mess of pottage?''

"It looks that way, Dad. Sorry to explode the family tradition."

I told Bruce to get two more opinions. He did. Both confirmed the earlier report. The family treasure was worthless.

All those years of caring, protecting, preserving and defending the family treasure—only to find it, along with the precious tradition it represented, was all phony!

We decided to return the coin to the safe-deposit box while we made up our minds what to do. Over the next few weeks I wondered how many of the other treasures I was hanging onto would prove to be junk if exposed to the light of truth.

During that time a theology professor wrote me, offended that I had suggested to a couple that they should leave their denomination. Actually, I had not advised them to leave the denomination. I advised them to use the same procedure used by the apostles in the first century to test whether they were where they should be. I advised them to speak their beliefs boldly and if the denomination received them, good. If they were rejected, they should leave in peace.

"There are few things sadder," the professor wrote, "than the person who jettisons all the old ecclesiastical baggage of denominationalism only to find they now have a pervading sense of rootlessness."

Rootlessness. I knew the sad feeling. But the mere fact that a thing has lasted a long time does not make it genuine.

Take our family treasure for instance.

"Dad," Bruce said one evening, "our coin was worth a lot more to our family before we had it checked by an expert."

That's true. On the other hand, I'm glad I didn't wait until I really needed $1,925 before we sold the coin.

I remember the eighty-four-year-old woman who wrote me after having read my biography of Kathryn Kuhlman, *Daughter of Destiny*. She was upset, saying it would have been better had I not told the truth. As a result of my book, she said, she had lost her salvation.

I wrote her back saying this was the greatest thing that could have happened to her. At least now she knew she was lost. Before, she was like me with my gold coin—believing something that wasn't so.

We finally made a decision. Only a fool holds on to something that is not real. I gave Bruce the green light to sell the coin since it did have a trace of gold in it. He took it back to the collector and sold it for $79.

But it wasn't a total loss. The copper matchbox, it seems, had once belonged to General Grant. Since it was in perfect condition it brought almost $1,000.

Sometimes you find your treasures in the strangest places.

The Tidal Waves Are Coming—Maybe

There are few sensations to match waking up at 4 a.m. and realizing your house is being shaken by an earthquake. I mean, a fellow could get downright religious at a time like that.

Most Floridians have never experienced an earthquake; that is, unless they moved to Florida from California, which very few people do since the nation is tilted westward and loose things always roll downhill. However, I had just returned from New Guinea where I had gone through a real live, teeth-jarring, road-buckling, mountain-toppling *guria*. To be at home in what I thought was the safest place in the world, my Florida bed, and suddenly feel the same sensations caused me no little mind-searching.

Now aside from the fact that a host of prophecies was confirmed that morning (one of them being a long-standing California prophecy that one day everything *east* of the San Andreas Fault would break off and slide into the sea) and a lot more came into being, our family did learn some things from that mini-quake which rocked our house for a few seconds.

It forced us to think about the importance of material things. I mean, if you have thirty seconds to get out of your house before it is swallowed up in a yawning chasm, it seems good to plan ahead what you would try to salvage.

In an after-dinner conference the next evening, I allowed each child the privilege of deciding on two things to take with them in case they had to leap for safety in the middle of the night. (My wife had already declared, pragmatically, that she'd take her houserobe and glasses.)

The children opted for things like their Bibles (I suspected that was to please me); an almost-completed school research paper; and the cat, Mrs. Robinson. I stated this was a waste of time because it is impossible to catch Mrs. Robinson in thirty seconds.

Our daughter Sandy said she would not leave unless she could take the twenty-seven stuffed animals she sleeps with every night. When I reminded her she was limited to two things, she said she'd take her mom and me. That was such a nice thought, even if we were second to the stuffed animals, that I declared I'd clear the table. The children headed for the TV room while Mom took the flashlight and went out to inspect the yard—just in case a yawning chasm might be appearing in the flower bed.

Written prophecies have always intrigued me—especially those which are printed into book form and become best-sellers. One famous prophecy, called simply *The Vision*, had the people in our church in a turmoil. Before reading it, they were having a wonderful time fellow-shipping with Catholics. Now this prophecy, which was selling by the millions, was telling them to keep their distance since the fire from heaven which would surely destroy all Catholics would get anyone standing close by as well. I did some quick mental calculations of what the royalty would be on a million books and told Jackie, "What we need are a few non-profit prophets."

For once, she agreed.

We had just finished reading two other printed prophecies. One was a dire warning of famines, earthquakes of unprecedented size and other disasters which would fall on America. The other predicted that Florida would break off and slide into the sea. The second "prophet," after mailing out her predictions, announced that it just so happened she had purchased property above the high water mark and for a reasonable price you could buy a lot and join her in total safety. That, it seemed to me, was the mark of a real entrepreneur. Why settle for the sale of a few books when you could piggyback on it with property sales at the same time?

She reminded me of my high school football coach who insisted every boy should wear a certain kind of football shoe. The shoe could be purchased only at the coach's sporting-goods store. I guess anti-trust laws can't be applied to prophets, however.

The question is not whether God is still speaking. The question is, Are we hearing correctly? Several years ago I woke in the middle of the night having heard what I knew was the "voice of God." It was time, the voice said, to syndicate my weekly newspaper column on a national basis. I lay awake the rest of the night, too excited to sleep.

The next day I began making plans. This was God's way, I realized, to get our financially strapped family out of debt. Quick calculations indicated I could soon be making several thousand dollars per week.

Prophecy, I knew, should always be submitted to other prophets for confirmation. I submitted this one to the elders of the church who confirmed my "word." They were especially supportive when I told them I would soon be able to support the church, rather than having the church support me.

My wife confirmed it. She saw it as a chance to keep me home.

My five children, excited that this would be a family business and I would put them all to work at top salaries, also gave enthusiastic confirmations. It's easy to confirm a prophecy that puts money in your pocket.

But that's where the confirmations stopped. America's newspapers were about as interested in my stuff as the pope is interested in a Jimmy Swaggart sermon. "Why don't you write a medical column?" one editor responded. "We've got a lot of readers who need help with their gout."

Another editor suggested I write a cooking column. Still another told me to drop dead.

But when God has spoken it's hard to back down. I spent more than $1,500 sending camera-ready samples—complete with stamped, self-addressed envelopes and a contract—to the 5,000 various editors in America. After six weeks, only two papers had accepted my column, and one of them said the only way they would run it was if I paid them $5 a week.

I wish I could report I am now America's favorite syndicated columnist. That God had taken my failure and turned it into a marvelous victory. Not so. I'm glad I tried. How else can you get something out of your system? But every time I hear someone say, "God told me to do it"— whether "it" is to write a book or run for president—I remember that voice in the night.

God does tell people to do things. But we need to realize there are a lot of other voices out there besides His. Some come from what my wife calls the P-I-T.

All this raises the question of all these last-days prophecies sweeping the world. Several years ago the nation was swamped with rumors of hitchhikers who got in people's cars, said that Jesus was coming soon and then disappeared. The hitchhikers ranged in appearance from bearded hippies to little old women in tennis shoes. The only trouble was, I never was able to talk to anyone who actually picked up one of these characters. It was always "a friend told me he had heard...."

Shortly afterwards there was a bevy of photographs that appeared. They were of a gowned and bearded figure surrounded by clouds. One woman told me the photo was taken by her aunt in Miami. Another was taken by a woman who spied the figure in the Nebraska clouds and leaped from her car just in time to snap the picture before "he" disappeared. Still another said the figure appeared over a Hawaiian volcano. All were the same photograph.

When I asked the people what the figure represented, they all said it was a warning that Christ was coming soon. I'm afraid I disappointed them with my lack of enthusiasm. The Bible gives us far more warning than signs in the sky. And even if I weren't skeptical of darkroom techniques, it bothers me that so many of us are gullible, looking for signs to titillate our emotions rather than trusting in the Word of God.

Next came the earthquake prophecies, starting with California and moving to Florida. These were followed by a rash of prophecies centering around the comet Kohoutek—which interestingly enough never did get close enough to be seen, much less cause the feared tidal waves which would show forth God's judgment.

Jesus said in the last days we would have false prophets, many performing great signs and wonders, saying of the coming Lord: "Behold, He is in the desert. Behold, He is in the secret chambers."

"Believe it or not," Jesus said (or at least that's what it would sound like if He said it today), "when I return you won't need a photograph to prove it."

Last year a frantic woman called our house in the middle of the night. She said she'd just received a call saying a giant tidal wave was about to engulf the state of Florida. What should she do?

I said, "Shout, 'Hallelujah!' If it's true, we'll all see Jesus before dawn. If it's not true, get me the name of the person who told you so I'll know whom not to believe. Either way—we win."

THREE

The Lord Is Just, the Lord Is Fair, He Gave Some Brains and Others Hair

Someone, quite without my knowledge or permission, has enrolled me in an organization known as Bald-Headed Men of America. I know because my packet of stuff arrived in the mail this morning.

I have a sneaking suspicion it was Brad Reed, a nearly thirty-year-old college student who lives in the neighborhood and is rapidly losing his own hair. Misery, I've discovered, genuinely craves company; if you can pull someone else down to your own level, things don't seem so bad.

Anyway, I am, it seems—although reluctantly, a member of the Bald-Headed Men of America (BHMA).

Back in 1972 a chrome-dome named John Capps in Dunn, North Carolina (P.O. Box B.A.L.D.), got tired of fighting the obvious. "If you don't have it, flaunt it," he said. He founded BHMA, which now

51

has over 18,000 members. Such famous baldies as sportscaster Joe Garagiola, actor Telly Savalas, "Love Boat" captain Gavin MacLeod and TV weatherman Willard Scott belong. So does former President Jerry Ford. Applications for membership have also been sent to famous toupee-wearers such as actor Burt "Billiardball" Reynolds and sportscaster Howard Cosell, but at last report they have not responded.

Capps, who is president of his own advertising and public relations firm, travels the country promoting his organization. Capitalizing on his own glabrous condition, he tells convention audiences:

> The Lord is just, the Lord is fair.
> He gave some brains and others hair.

Well, that may be funny to slick-headed folks like Capps, but for guys like me who weep every time they wash their hair and see all those fellows leaving home and disappearing down the drain—never again to be replaced—it's frustrating.

My first reaction on receiving my membership card was to call Brad and tell him he wasted his five-dollar membership fee on me. I'm not about to order a T-shirt even though I have a choice of three slogans:
- Bald Is Beautiful
- Slick Is Sexy
- Rub a Bald Head Tonight

Nor am I interested in the *Chrome-Dome Newsletter* (published every now and then). Despite the fact Jackie insisted I send off for one of their big lapel pins that say, "It's Hard to Be Humble When You Shine," I steadfastly refused to have anything to do with something as degrading and deplorable as BHMA.

Then I noticed that one of the privileges of belonging was the right to nominate other baldies to BHMA. Suddenly I was interested. Nominees, the application blank said, must have a bald spot, be a chrome-dome, wear a toupee or have a haircut with a hole in it. I quickly sat down and nominated four men I always suspected were bald, even though I had no way of proving it without sneaking up behind them and lifting their rug. They are:
- a former official in the Pentecostal Holiness Church now involved in ecumenical work;
- a nasal-toned televangelist who wears a big rose in his lapel;

- a bearded missionary evangelist who lives in Tulsa and spends a lot of time preaching in Africa;
- an Assembly of God traveling speaker who once pastored a big church in Florida.

Of course, there is no public evidence any of these mighty men of God has anything but a massive head of hair, but I have always suspected there was far less under their mops than appeared on the surface. Only their hairdressers—and their wives, and anybody who gets within fifty feet of them—really know.

A writer-friend of mine recently had a hair transplant. The old way was to take plugs of hair off the side of your head and patch them into the scalp like corn stalks. He paid a lot of money for the new way, which is to take long strips of hair from the back of his head and graft them to his bald scalp as a landscaper lays blocks of grass. He finally had to stop before his head was covered, however, because his ears were being pulled together behind his head like the rear pockets on a pair of pants with the waist shortened.

One thing is sure: Bald men are desperate to have hair. I'd like some, too, but I don't want it enough to go out and buy it. No matter how expensive the toupee, everyone always knows you're wearing it. I don't want someone else's wife saying about me what my wife says after we get in our car to drive home: "Did you know Bob wears a rug? (Snicker, snicker.)"

Besides, there is always that sneaking suspicion: Can you really trust a man who wears a wig? I mean, if he tries to deceive you with his appearance, what will he do with your money? Or your wife?

Sure, I've given thought to buying a wig. Every bald-headed man has. But then I wonder what would happen if I bent over and it fell off. Or if I turned my head real fast—and my hair stayed still.

I also nominated six non-wig-wearing baldies:
- California pastor Jack Hayford;
- Korean pastor Yonggi Cho;
- musician Phil Driscoll;
- evangelist Lester Sumrall;
- Charles Hunter, who is the backstage side of the Happy Hunter team.
- Bible teacher Tony Campolo, who likes to say to a crowd of young people, "What you're looking at is not a bald head but a solar battery

53

for a high-powered sex machine.''

My favorite wig-wearer is Marilyn Hickey's husband, Wally, who pastors the Happy Church in Denver. Wally once told me of an experience he had walking through the pitch-black Hezekiah's Tunnel in Jerusalem. This quarter-mile-long waterway, carved through solid rock far below the city wall, channels water from the Virgin's Spring to the Pool of Siloam inside the city.

Wally and a small group from his church were wading single-file through the narrow tunnel one afternoon. The water was unusually high—above the waist of the people—and each person was carrying a small candle. At one place, Wally banged his head on the low ceiling, dislodging his white-haired wig which fell into the flowing water. Before he could grab it, it had floated out of reach.

Suddenly there was a terrifying scream echoing through the tunnel. It came from a woman downstream who had looked down at the water in the light of her flickering candle to see what it was that had brushed against her bosom. Seeing the white wig swimming around her body, she went bonkers. Pandemonium broke loose in the dark tunnel as the panic spread to the others standing single-file in flowing water. Cries of ''Snake!,'' ''Rats!'' and ''Demons!'' echoed off the ancient walls.

Wally finally had to out-shout everyone and holler, ''It's just my wig!'' By that time the wig was far downstream and the terrified people finally made their way out of the tunnel into the welcomed sunlight where they found Wally's wig floating serenely in the Pool of Siloam.

One wag later remarked it was a good thing this took place in the twentieth century rather than in Jesus' day. If the blind man Jesus sent to the Pool of Siloam to wash the mud from his eyes had received his sight and suddenly seen that white wig floating in the water, he probably would have gone blind again.

Anyway, thank God for Wally Hickey who doesn't seem to mind. Somehow, being in the company of these distinguished baldies—wigged or not—makes me feel better.

''If I can't grow it, I'll buy it,'' Pastor Harold Hardisty told me. But Harold was a good sport. On some Sundays he'd wear his hairpiece, but if the wind was blowing he'd just as soon show up in the pulpit without it. I loved it the morning he, in the course of his sermon, actually took his wig off and laid it on top of the piano to illustrate his point about hiding your light under a bushel.

That's what's refreshing about TV weatherman Willard Scott, who one day wears a toupee, as a man would put on a necktie, and the next day appears on NBC bald as a billiard ball. Such freedom can get even a faltering network good ratings.

There's an irony to all this which still mystifies me. A number of years ago I decided to let my hair grow long. I mean really long. Like down to my shoulders. At the time I thought I had just been "set free" by the Holy Spirit. Now, in looking back on it, I'm not sure the Holy Spirit ever sets you free to make a dunce out of yourself. I think I probably did it for the same reason fifty-year-old men have affairs with twenty-five-year-old women: It's your last chance to prove you can still do it, although in my case the only place I could do it was down the back of my neck. The rest of my hair had already departed for greener pastures.

In my case it was pure ego. Hair was the symbol of my manhood—and my independence. In looking back on that strange period in my life, I understand why some of today's public leaders are so touchy about their physical appearance, especially their hair. (I know one be-wigged pastor who refuses to kneel at his own altar for fear someone might come along, lay hands on him and inadvertently lift his toupee.)

In my case it was not a matter of going out and buying it; it was, instead, if you can't grow it on top, grow it on the sides.

It was not one of the better periods of my life. I keep the photographs just to remind me that God will let you do anything you want to—even make a fool out of yourself.

I wore it long for two years. I looked like a straight-haired Phil Driscoll (he who blows the trumpet with the breath of angels)—with just enough on top to keep the sun from reflecting too brightly. There was an additional problem: Not only was my hair thinning, but the individual hairs were fine like corn silk. So when I turned my head quickly my hair would swirl around in front of my face. I was constantly touching it with my hands, trying to push it back where it belonged. During that entire two-year period I never did get used to the unfamiliar sensation of having hair around my ears and down the back of my neck. The only ones who approved were my teenage daughters. The rest of the world in which I lived thought I was either a bit weird or was on the verge of leaving my wife for a twenty-five-year-old woman.

Pensacola pastor Ken Sumrall, the only man who spoke truth to me during that strange wilderness wandering, said I was like the fellow in his church who had just enough religion to keep him from sinning, but not enough to keep him from wanting to. In other words, he was innoculated against the world—but not immune. I concluded that Ken (who has never tried to hide his baldness) meant I was too honest to buy a toupee and too vain to let my head go natural—so I had gone crazy instead.

I honestly don't know why I let it grow long, but I do know why I finally cut it off.

In the first place, I hated to wash it every day. My long-haired daughters washed theirs and then, to dry it, would turn down the air-conditioning thermostat, go outside and sit in front of the compressor while it blew hot air. I was too proud to do that, of course. In spite of the fact I looked like a cross between Timothy Leary and Walt Disney's Goofy, I refused to join them every morning before school, sitting cross-legged in the yard next to the air-conditioning unit, hair flying in the wind. So I had to get up extra early and spend the time in the bathroom washing and drying. I hated it. But when you are vain, you do all sorts of things you hate.

Reason number two was the wind. I never could figure out how the long-haired guys kept their hair neat without a hairnet. Once indoors I was safe—unless somebody opened a window or turned on a fan, and I had to be careful at church meetings not to sit under an air-conditioner vent. But outside I was constantly having to walk sideways or keep my hands on top of my head. It reached a climax before Christmas when I took my family to the theater. The wind was blowing like crazy so I had to enter the theater walking backwards. The usher thought I was trying to pull the old con game of walking in backwards so he would think I was leaving and not ask for my ticket. After the confusion died down, he apologized in a loud voice saying, "I'm sorry, madam."

Jackie bought me a huge can of hairspray. ("If you're going to look like a woman you might as well start using women's products.") Besides the blow to my masculinity, hairspray presented another problem. I quickly discovered if it got the slightest bit damp (say you're caught in a shower or get hit by a water sprinkler), it would set up like concrete.

Only a shampoo could undo the damage. Once, after getting my hair wet changing planes, I had to shampoo in the tiny rest room of a DC-9 on a short flight between Atlanta and Charlotte. I spilled water all over the front of my trousers and used two rolls of paper towels and a box of Kleenex trying to dry my hair before we landed. By then the flight attendant was banging on the door of the rest room wanting to know if I was OK.

The final blow came when Jackie's hairdresser, Lou Brodrick, approached me after a church service and offered to trim my hair. Me? Sitting in a woman's beauty parlor? That was for fags and television evangelists—not macho backwoodsmen like me. But looking in the mirror, I knew I needed help if I was to keep what I had. Besides, I hadn't been into the backwoods in fifteen years.

The next Sunday I pulled Lou aside and said if she could arrange a time after dark, I'd let her do it. We agreed on Tuesday night after the shop was closed. I sneaked into the beauty parlor and sat in the chair while she put a sheet around my neck and clamps in my long, blond locks. Just at that exact minute the door burst open and the church gossip, Gloria Grapevine, came rushing back into the shop to get her purse. She took one look at me, gasped and then burst into hilarious laughter before running back out into the night.

That did it. I pulled off the sheet, thanked Lou and went home. I marched straight to the bathroom, got Jackie's scissors out of the drawer and went to work like Delilah on Samson. Unlike the Bible strongman, however, I was regaining my lost manhood—not losing it. Bald may or may not be beautiful—but it's real.

Sure, I wish I had locks like James Robison or John Wimber. (Please, please, don't write and say you have secret information they wear toupees. A man needs to look up to someone who's genuine.) But reality says I am balding—and one day may be bald. That's the reason folks like John Capps and BHMA have their place in the kingdom. They keep us real, honest and laughing at ourselves.

Capps says the Lord made millions and millions of heads, and those He was ashamed of He covered. He also believes that bald is neater, more distinguished. Best of all, he states, most intelligent and good-looking women love a bald head—just to kiss it, touch it, rest their little fingers on it.

You'll never convince me that's so. Even though it's good for jokes ("I used Rinse Away and it worked"), I still wish I had hair. And that's the bare fact.

On the other hand, there are distinct advantages that those of us with thinning hair have over those brutes who have as thick and luxuriant a growth as the primates in the city zoo. I've been watching a certain fellow who works out at the same racquetball club where I play. After an hour on the court we both come into the locker room at the same time, shower, towel off and get dressed. Then, while I'm packing my gear in my bag to leave, he goes back into the bathroom to go through his post-shower ritual. I stayed one afternoon just to time him. He spent fifteen minutes using a blower and a brush to dry and shape his beautiul hair.

He works out three times a week. That means he spends forty-five minutes a week doing his hair. And that's only in the club locker room. I assume he does the same at home at least six mornings a week (although guys this vain usually fix their hair on their day off as well). That means he spends 135 minutes a week on his hair. Two hours and fifteen minutes.

Simple arithmetic shows he could be spending almost ten twelve-hour days a year messing with his locks. Multiply this by twenty years, at which time surely he will begin to look like me, and you see that his vanity has consumed six and one half months of his daytime life. Six and one half months rubbing in mousse, blowing hot air at his hair, squirting it with hair spray, and primping it with a comb or brush. Not to mention the cost of equipment, supplies, electricity and the really big item—haircuts and styling.

Maybe I'm not so bad off after all. I haven't spent a dime on haircuts since 1972 when I purchased one of those little plastic combs that holds a razor blade. I figure I've saved almost $2,500 in that department alone—not to mention the two and a half weeks I would have spent in the barber's chair during that period of time.

Not only that, I never have to carry bulky hairblowers, brushes, bottles of conditioner and sprays when I travel. All I need is a piece of soap, a towel and a comb—which sees only occasional use. In fact, one of those miniature plastic containers of shampoo—the kind they supply in the bathrooms of fancy hotels—will last me for a week.

When you stop and think about it, hair is really irrelevant. The fact is, we no longer need it. It's something nature provided countless centuries ago to keep us warm when we crawled out of the cave. Now, thanks to hats, helmets, sunscreen and roofs, hair is merely decorative. In many ways we're better off without it.

Thinning hair or a bald spot has never prevented anyone from being who God intended for him to be. Bald-headed men elicit trust and are more intelligent-looking.

In fact, I have long believed that Jesus Himself was bald, although artists' renditions of a chrome-dome Jesus have yet to be seen. Sadly, when I mention my theory of a bald-headed Jesus, people treat me the same way they treat people who deny the virgin birth or don't believe in the rapture.

Recently a plethora of new drugs and medications has hit the market—all guaranteed to grow hair. The best known is Minoxidil, which supposedly has been putting hair on bald Canadians for years, but it has not been allowed across the border. Before a similar product was introduced in this country a total of seventy-two bald-headed men were arrested in Vancouver trying to cross back into the United States with the wonder drug hidden in their luggage. One innovative man had a quart of the chemical sealed in a plastic bag which fit snugly under his toupee. Another carried the drug in three old Wildroot Hair Tonic bottles. Discerning customs officials quickly spotted him as a smuggler, of course, when he took off his hat and they saw he was bald.

Three baldies actually made it across Lake Ontario from Toronto to Buffalo in a rubber raft carrying 134 plastic milk jugs filled with Minoxidil.

The most innovative smuggling operation was the one carried out by trapeze and highwire artists known as the Bald Eagles. The three-man team, consisting of a hairless father and two bald sons, smuggled ninety gallons of Minoxidil from Canada to the United States during a performance at Niagara Falls on July 4. The Eagles rode bicycles on a high wire across the Canadian Falls while balancing thirty-gallon garbage cans on their heads. What was in the garbage cans? You guessed it. Contraband Minoxidil. Customs officials, who could not prove their case, estimated the street value of the illegal drug was more than $1.5 million.

All this simply points to how desperate baldies are to have hair. I want it, too, but not bad enough to sink any more money into "grow hair" schemes. Take Minoxidil, for instance. A month's supply costs $100—even in Canada. Moreover, a user must continue to apply the lotion daily. When treatments stop, hair falls out again. And, according to *U.S. News and World Report*, "when physicians set up a controlled test, they were amazed to find that hair grew on individuals given a supposedly inert mixture of ingredients as well as those given the drug. 'It was just one of those strange, serendipitous results that we can't explain yet,' said one researcher, who asked not to be named lest his corporate sponsors be angered."

Last year a nutritionist in our church gave me a full case of something called "Nutri-Gain," which is also "guaranteed to grow hair." I applied it religiously as the instructions said. Every morning for three months, then twice a week until the supply ran out, I mixed the ingredients and rubbed the mess into my bald scalp. Aside from causing me to smell like rotten eggs, I could notice no difference. I had my wife stand on the cedar chest at the foot of our bed and take before-and-after pictures, looking straight down at my bald head as I sat cross-legged on the bedroom floor. Nothing. Not a single new hair as far as I could tell. There was an interesting side effect, however. Huge amounts of hair began to grow out of my ears, and twice I thought I noticed hair growing in the palm of my hand. I decided it was time to stop the treatment and resolve myself to the fact I was going to be just like my father—bald.

I take courage in the fact that a number of Bible heroes were bald. Take Elisha, for one. He proved God blesses baldness by showing it's dangerous to make fun of bald-headed prophets. Feel sorry for us. Ignore us. But don't tease us. We're protected by she-bears. Just remember what happened to those forty-two juvenile delinquents from Bethel who came running out to jeer at Elisha.

When was the last time, by the way, you heard a sermon based on 2 Kings 2:23—especially by some mop-headed preacher who is always complaining about the price of razor cuts?

And what about Absalom, that long-haired, hippie son of David? If he'd been bald he might have been king. But while fleeing from David's army on a horse, his long hair caught in the low limbs of a tree and left him dangling in the air. Tradition says he was speared to death by three bald-headed soldiers.

You see, rejection runs deep for some of us—especially when we've been rejected by something as prominent as our hair. And despite the fact I think I have adjusted rather well to my physical state, there are still times when I dream of sitting back in the barber's chair and letting him slosh good old Wildroot or Vitalis on my wavy locks. But those days, like so many other things in life, are gone with the wind.

The best I can do is look at my old high-school annual pictures and sigh. Bald is beautiful? Not on your depilated dome, John Capps. The only advantages (aside from being able to comb your head with a Kleenex) are spiritual. It's good to know that the Lord, who numbers hairs on heads, doesn't have to work very hard when it comes to me. And I hope when I get my new body in heaven, His words will have literal meaning: "Well done, good and faithful servant: thou hast been faithful over a few things, I will make thee ruler over many."

FOUR

Pastoral Ministry, or You Can Fool Most of the Folks Most of the Time

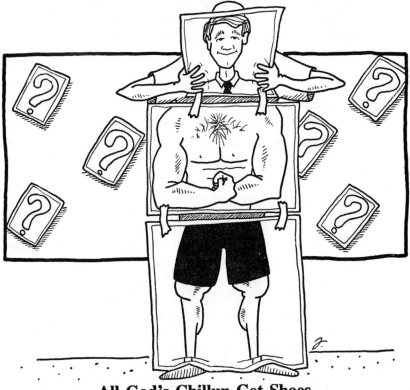

All God's Chillun Got Shoes

It wasn't too many years ago that any man who appeared in public wearing patent leather shoes was suspect. I mean, it wasn't safe to sit beside him in the bus station. But times have changed. Despite my contention that only televangelists and the piano player in the gospel quartet wore patent leather shoes, I finally gave in to my wife's exasperated appeals and consented to buy a pair of shiny, black patent leather loafers.

For two years Jackie nagged me about my old, scuffed mail-order shoes. "It's bad enough that you insist on wearing sneakers to church here at home," she complained. "But I'm ashamed to travel with you out of town. If you're not wearing your jogging shoes, you're wearing those twelve-year-old $7.95 specials made out of plastic. All your friends look nice when they speak at conferences. But you look as if you've just ridden into town on a load of turnips. Look at Bob Mumford, Morris Sheats and James Beall. They're strong and masculine—and they wear patent leather shoes. You need to present a better image.''

It's not that I objected to a better image. I just hate it when people compare me with other people who are obviously more successful than I am. My mother used to do this. "Why can't you dress nice like your brother, Clay? He's so neat and orderly."

Now my wife had taken over, comparing me with successful preachers and traveling evangelists who obviously had enough money to buy flashy shoes. Why couldn't she understand that I hate new shoes? They pinch my feet and make me walk as if I have some kind of groin deformity. Besides, it was hard for me to believe that shiny shoes would make me look more masculine.

Then, without my knowledge, Jackie got to a friend of mine who ran a shoe store. One Sunday morning he approached me after church— the time I am most vulnerable. I had just preached a pathetic sermon: the kind you realize in the middle that no one is listening to, and besides, you don't know what you're talking about. I was moping around the front of the auditorium wondering why nobody wanted to talk to me when he stepped up and made me the kind of offer I couldn't refuse.

"If you'll throw away those old clodhoppers," he said, "I'll give you a brand-new pair of shoes. All you have to do is send your wife in and let her pick them out. No charge."

There are two things I hate more than wearing new shoes: one is paying for them; the other is picking them out. He had hit me at my weakest spot. I knew she would pick out a pair of shiny ones, but since the price was right, how could I object?

The following afternoon, after Jackie made her visit to the shoe store, we left to attend the National Leadership Conference in North Carolina. All the big guns were going to be there, and I was the opening night speaker. Jackie looked forward to my new image.

She put her foot down when I tried to pack my tennis shoes. "You've got all those nice things and never wear them. Furthermore," she insisted, "I want you to wear your new shoes on the plane."

It was my first time to try them on. Even though they were the correct size, they gripped my feet like vises. "They'll loosen up after you've worn them awhile,'' Jackie assured me as I hobbled through the departure lounge at the Melbourne Airport.

By the time we reached Atlanta, however, the pain was excruciating. We had to change planes, and I limped into the terminal. While Jackie made a trip to the rest room, I collapsed into a chair. Anger, like molten lava, was boiling inside me. How could I possibly preach that night with my feet hurting so? If only I had brought my comfortable old shoes. No, I had to be a Mr. Milquetoast, pushed around by my wife.

A guy walked by. He was wearing tennis shoes—and whistling. It was more than I could stand. It was all Jackie's fault, her and her desire to improve my image and make me wear Mumford shoes. Well, image be hanged if it caused my feet to suffer untold agony.

By the time Jackie returned I was ready to explode. Before I could say a word, however, she pointed to my foot. ''What's that piece of paper sticking out of your shoe?''

I had a sinking feeling in the pit of my stomach. I quickly put my hand over the area and stammered, ''It's nothing.''

Now she was giggling. ''Take your shoes off.''

I resisted but finally pulled them off. To my utter mortification, I found I had failed to remove the cardboard liners. I felt my face turn cherry red as I sheepishly pulled out the thick cardboard and replaced my shoes on my feet.

Ah! Comfort!

That night I entered the auditorium on the arm of my wife—wearing not only a coat and tie, but my flashy, new patent leather pumps. Surprisingly enough, my only concern was that some tennis-shoe-wearing clod might step on them and leave scratches.

The Jesus Look

Remember when it was ''in'' and ''chic'' and ''right on'' to grow a beard? That was back during the time when women wore long dresses and the Jesus Movement was rushing at us from the West Coast like tremors from a Los Angeles earthquake.

For some of us, it was an excuse to do what we'd always wanted to do but were too proper. So at forty years of age I grew my first beard.

''It's time I started looking like Jesus,'' I told my wife.

"It's also time you started practicing celibacy," Jackie said pointedly. "If you had grown that thing fifteen years ago we'd only have one child rather than five."

I took heart, however, in that many others I knew were also growing beards for the first time. All told me they were doing it to be like Jesus. Jim McKeever, one of the nation's top financial analysts and sometime preacher, not only grew a beard but he changed his name from Jim to James and wrote a book about being like Jesus. Now that's real commitment.

Granted, my beard wasn't what I expected. I mean, it didn't make me look like the man in the Hathaway shirt, much less like Jesus. I'm not sure what Jesus looked like, but I had a hard time picturing Him looking like James McKeever—or me: a middle-aged, overweight, balding Anglo-Saxon with a beard that made me look thirty years older than I was.

Had it been just one color it wouldn't have been so bad. But it was multicolored: mostly gray with tinges of red, brown and yellow. Also, it didn't grow straight down like Robert E. Lee's beard. It grew in many directions—mostly out—like a scared porcupine.

I never did get used to it. Not that it bothered me. In fact, I scarcely knew it was there unless I caught a random look at myself as I passed some store window—which usually caused me to jump out into the middle of the street in terror that I was being attacked by a mugger.

The problem was the way it affected other people. Like the night I attended a small dinner party. When I walked into the room it was as though I had appeared dressed in a coat of mail, or with charcoal smeared over my face. The people, none of whom had seen me since I began to look like Jesus, tried to ignore it—the same way they ignore a man who has a huge pimple on his nose or a big glob of mustard on his chin. They kept staring, yet whenever I looked up at them, they rapidly turned their heads and talked to people who weren't even there.

People couldn't seem to keep their eyes off my chin when I talked with them. One woman stood it as long as she could, then broke into gales of laughter right in the middle of one of my most profound points. "I'm sorry," she said, spitting her drink all over the front of my shirt, "but when you lick your lips it looks like a groundhog sticking his head out of the grass to see if the sun's shining."

Bending double in laughter, she staggered away. It was terribly disconcerting—especially when I was trying so hard to look like Jesus.

Then there were the silly remarks. Older women had a way of pointing at me from far off and squealing, "Ohhh, here comes Ernest Hemingway."

Younger women would giggle and throw up their hands in mock defense. "Ohhh, don't kiss me with that fuzzy thing." (As if I even intended to try.)

Beardless men would sneer.

Bearded men followed me closely with their eyes as I passed, no doubt comparing my style and shape with their own and asking themselves those universal questions:

"I wonder if he shaves his neck?" (I did.)

"I wonder if he dyed it gray on purpose?" (I didn't.)

"I wonder if he uses mascara on his mustache?" (I refuse to answer.)

"I wonder if he has insects living in it, as I do in mine?" (Absolutely not!)

"I wonder if his wife lets him kiss her, or has he taken an involuntary vow of chastity as most bearded men are forced to do?" (Anyone who follows Jesus has to sacrifice.)

Only the children, including my own, reacted positively. In their open innocence they did things like putting their hands on my face and rubbing them up and down, or saying things like, "I like it. It makes you look so handsome."

It's no wonder Jesus put children on His knee.

My own mother, when she first saw it, put both hands over her face, leaving only a tiny space between her fingers for me to kiss her on the cheek. Later she yanked it—hard. (Why would anyone, especially an eighty-year-old mother, want to yank the beard of a man trying to look like Jesus?) She said she wanted to find out if it was real.

My mother-in-law, who had grown exceedingly tolerant of my strange ways, squealed and said, "Ohhh, you look just like Burl Ives." Then when she saw I was sorely wounded, she softened the blow by adding, "I mean your stomach, not that awful-looking beard."

My wife, who finally said she approved, comforted me in my times of rejection by saying encouraging things like, "I've always wondered what it was like being married to Moses. Now I know."

Others interrupted serious conversations with questions like, "Does it itch?" or "What do you do when you have to blow your nose through that mustache?"

One good friend asked, "Why are you doing it—growing the beard, I mean?"

Tired of saying I was trying to look like Jesus, I paraphrased the answer the old preacher, Charles Spurgeon, gave when someone asked him why he smoked a cigar. "I'm growing it for the glory of God."

I can still hear my friend laughing as he staggered away.

It took my father twice as long as it did me to grow any facial hair. While I grew my first beard when I was forty, my father waited until he was eighty to grow his first mustache. "I've always wanted to know what I'd look like with a mustache," he said. "But your mother said she would never kiss a man with facial hair. At eighty that doesn't bother me anymore, so I'm going to do it."

He kept it for four years then shaved it off. "It just wasn't me," he said.

My beard didn't last that long. I kept it less than a year. Maybe when I'm eighty and don't mind looking like Moses—and don't mind not being kissed—I'll try again. In the meantime, Jackie suggested that I forget trying to look like Jesus. Unlike me, she simply can't picture Jesus with a bald head.

Your True Image on a Glossy Black-and-White Five-by-Seven

Many magazines and newspapers have a policy of running pictures of their writers and columnists next to their copy. Readers, the concept goes, like to know what the writer looks like.

It helps, for instance, to know that newspaper columnist Mike Royko, the Chicago whino, has the look of an aging bald eagle; that George Will of *Newsweek* actually looks like a scholarly, dry wit; and that Stephen Strang, my editor at *Charisma*, does not fit the stereotype of all other editors and wear a green eye shade and have soup stains all over his tie as I've sometimes falsely accused him.

On the other hand, my picture, which goes alongside my Last Word column in *Charisma*, has not had the effect on my readers I had hoped.

Indeed, it has had quite the opposite effect.

One woman, who wrote the editor threatening to cancel her subscription unless they stopped running my picture, said I looked like her first husband, who smiled politely every time he hit her with his fist.

Another man wrote, saying, "If that man's a preacher, our nation's in a lot of trouble."

Another said he'd "be satisfied just to know that that preacher's a man."

Nothing seems to work for me. Some people always look good in a photo. Others seem to know just what to do to look photogenic. They know how to smile into the camera, or better, how to look wistfully at a spider on the wall. They know they photograph better from one side than the other. They know to check their coat to see if it has bunched up around their ears and not to bend forward so their bald spot shows and not to freeze in one of those rectangular "say cheese" smiles they learned to do in the third grade.

Charisma magazine spent a lot of money trying to get a picture of me that looked halfway decent. They tried me with a coat and tie, and everyone almost died laughing. Next they took dozens of shots of me in a turtleneck sweater to try to hide my wrinkled neck. All that did was make me look like a turtle rather than the hoped-for Robert Redford image. They tried pictures with me wearing a hat to hide my bald head. Next I was forced to pose with my hand on my chin, like that famous statue of the Greek thinker sitting naked on a rock wondering how he was going to explain to his wife why he was coming home from the office party without any clothes on.

"Have you ever seen a picture of Iverna Tompkins?" an exasperated Steve Strang asked me. "She always has her hand on her chin. It makes her look thoughtful."

"That's because she's biting a hangnail, not looking thoughtful," I argued.

So the magazine has alternated between running a cartoon drawing and my high school football picture.

Pictures fool you. Take the one of Pat Robertson—sitting in front of all those books with his legs crossed and his coat buttoned. It's no wonder the people in the South didn't vote for him on Super Tuesday. What kind of man can sit in a chair with his legs crossed and keep his coat buttoned at the same time? No normal man, I'll tell you that.

A friend of mine who works for a Washington, D.C., newspaper said the order came down from "the top" that every photograph of President Reagan should be made from a slanted angle—looking up at his chin. The old editor, who was angered that Reagan was the most photogenic man ever to live in the White House, was determined to prove to his readers that the president was really a wrinkled old man. So he instructed his photographers always to shoot from an angle that would highlight the wrinkles in Reagan's neck.

And who can forget those pictures of Jimmy Swaggart, weeping profusely into the camera? Or Tammy Faye Bakker with all that horrible makeup? Or Jim Bakker, smiling into the camera and looking all the world like Howdy Doody? None was a true representation—but we remember only what the photographs show.

That's the reason I keep trying to find a photo that makes me look the way I really am—a Robert Redford face mounted on the body of Arnold Schwarzenegger.

The biggest disillusionment comes when someone who's known you only through your picture sees you face to face.

Last week I walked into a local department store to buy a bathing suit. I was honored when the pretty young clerk recognized my name.

"I've read two of your books," she said, "and I always read the Last Word first in *Charisma*."

However, when I told her I needed a "large" I saw her face fall. "Gee," she said, "I thought you were skinny by looking at your picture."

"My face is skinny," I groaned, "but they couldn't get the rest of me into the camera lens."

Such is the fate of meeting a writer face to face. It's like discovering John Wayne had training wheels on his horse or that Sylvester Stallone wears built-up shoes.

I know the feeling. It's the same one I had when I discovered that Andy of the original "Amos 'n' Andy" was white and that Burt Reynolds wore a wig. Some disappointments are just too deep to put into words.

Not too long ago I was speaking in Norfolk when a lady came up to the speaker's platform. She had one of my books in her hand and said, "I want Mr. Buckingham's autograph. Which one is he?"

"Right here," the emcee said, nodding at me.

"Him?" the woman blurted out. "You're kidding!"

Unfortunately, I had just shaved off my Hemingway beard because I never could convince people it wasn't a briar patch that I had stuck to my face with peanut butter. Had I kept it, I'm sure her impression would have been different. But it did leave me wondering if writers shouldn't be people of mystery who regard reality as a nice place to visit but wouldn't want to live there. They should be a little weird and a lot unconventional. They should be wild, unpredictable, wear trench coats and sneer when they talk to women.

They should also never have their picture appear on their book jackets or alongside their magazine columns—especially if they're bald, misshapen and have wrinkled necks.

There's one thing they'll never be able to say about me, though. They'll never see me sitting in front of a bunch of books with my legs crossed and my coat buttoned. Never.

Pastor, Parson, Brother, Friend— But Please Don't Call Me Reverend

All the men in the Buckingham family had some kind of earned title— all but me. My two older brothers were men of great distinction: one, a Ph.D., was chairman of the Department of Industrial Management at Georgia Tech; the other, a West Point graduate, was a major general in the Army. My younger brother, with degrees from three great universities, was a medical doctor.

That made me look pretty plain when my name appeared along with theirs. But it never bothered me as much as it bothered my mother, who always suspected I would never quite measure up.

Titles had always been important to those on my mother's side of the family. My maternal grandfather was a "Kentucky Colonel"—back before the term was debased by the fried-chicken people. "Granted by the governor himself," my mother used to tell us children when talking of the distinguished old Southern gentleman with the gray hair, handlebar mustache and glossy mahogany cane. I never knew him by any name but Colonel Thompson.

Thus when I finished my formal schooling with a seminary degree, my mother's side of the family immediately began searching for some

71

way to title me. Shortly after graduation—while I was still driving a city bus for the Ft. Worth Transit Company—I began getting letters from my mother's side of the family addressed to The Reverend Jamie Buckingham.

I wrote back and asked not to be addressed that way. Why shouldn't my relatives just address me the way they always had—by my name? After all, I was still their cousin and nephew, and more important, their brother in Christ.

Shortly afterwards I started getting mail addressed to "Bro. Jamie Buckingham," as if Bro. were a title like Rev., Dr. or Gen.

But there is a distinct difference between titles earned and titles bestowed. Generals and doctors earn their titles.

But reverends?

Actually there is but one place in the entire Bible where the term "reverend" is used, and that is in reference to God Himself: "Holy and reverend is HIS name" (Psalm 111:9, KJV). Thus it always seemed slightly presumptuous for me to try to share the glory with Him.

Yet there was always that nagging feeling that I needed some kind of title in order to have status. I was constantly getting letters from people who had strings of degrees after their names. Some even signed their letters using their titles: Doctor, Reverend or Father. Others would sign their names and put their degree initials after it: "Sister Annie Mendoza, D.D." It all depended on how much status they needed.

I keep thinking about those conference registration forms you fill out that have a little place to check before you write your name: ( ) Mr., ( ) Miss, ( ) Mrs., ( ) Rev., ( ) Other. If you're a man you're either a Mr., a Rev. or an Other. I'd often wanted to check Other but was afraid some federal agency might get hold of it and start an investigation about my sexual orientation. So I just stick with Mr.

A friend recently introduced me to her fiance, a shy young man who had just been ordained into the Episcopal priesthood. "Jamie, this is Father Johnson."

Why, I asked myself, was she free to call me by my first name but felt compelled to refer to her fiance as "Father"? Granted, my children (and, shudder, now my wife) call me "Daddy." But that's a title earned—not conferred.

Clergymen, who should be the most secure people on earth, seem to be more title conscious than any others. I know a minister who never calls his wife anything but "Sister Hawthorne" in public. It makes me wonder how their pillow talk must go once the lights are turned out in the bedroom.

"Good night, Sister Hawthorne."

"Sweet dreams, Reverend dear."

Actually, the term "reverend" means "worthy of reverence." It referred to an exalted office in the church, much as judges on the bench are called "your honor." It is not a biblical title. But as clergymen elevated themselves from the original role of servant to that of master, titles were used to designate ascending functionaries: The Reverend, The Most Reverend, The Most Holy Reverend.

It seems the Man of Galilee was never concerned about titles or proper recognitions. Others referred to Him as Rabbi, Teacher, Master or Lord. When the title-conscious functionaries of the Sanhedrin insisted on titling Him, He said simply, "Call Me Son of Man." It was His way of saying, "You are the ones who need titles, not I."

Then all my theories got blown out of the water when I was offered— and accepted—an honorary doctor's degree from a Christian university.

"I told you not to poke fun at people with honorary degrees," Jackie said. "Now you have one yourself."

I was just glad it was a doctor of humane letters (D.H.L.) rather than a doctor of divinity (D.D.)—which would have made me sound like a Christmas candy.

"What's your degree in?"

"Divinity."

"With or without walnuts? Har! Har!"

My father used to quote poetry about honorary degrees.

> There was a young preacher named Tweedle,
> Who refused to accept his degree.
> It's bad enough being Tweedle,
> Without being Tweedle, D.D.

It wasn't until I got home from the graduation service and started to hang my certificate on the wall that I noticed the degree was misspelled. It says—big as life in black calligraphy on sheepskin—Doctor of *Human* Letters.

"God knew if you ever got an honorary degree you'd be impossible to live with," Jackie laughed. "So He gave you one and misspelled the title so you can't brag about it."

I felt like the fellow who won the humble button at the annual church awards banquet, only to have it taken from him the minute he put it on.

"Chickens," my wife loves to remind me, "have a way of coming home to roost."

On occasion, I try to picture how those early Christians addressed one another. Somehow it just seems out of character for the Reverend Doctor Bartholomew to announce a meeting in the catacombs, saying, "The Most Reverend James the Just will speak following the burnings in the colosseum."

So why not just stick to Mister, or even better, first names? The term "reverend" is an adjective, and an adjective I'm not. I'm not even a past participle. I'm a noun.

Besides, as Vance Havner used to say: it doesn't do any good to stick a label on an empty bottle.

So if you want to give me a really biblical title, just call me St. Jamie.

An Officer and a Gentleman

When I started my college ROTC training to become a U.S. Army officer, I was taught by men of proud tradition that there were three things a uniformed officer never did in public.

He never pushed a baby carriage.

He never carried an umbrella.

And I've forgotten the third thing.

I welcomed the tradition about pushing baby buggies. It didn't go with my image of masculinity, anyway.

When our first child was born, my parents gave us an ancient British perambulator, or "pram" for short. It was black, the size of a baby bed, and mounted on four huge wire-spoked, rubber-tired wheels—complete with springs and shock absorbers. And it had a convertible top which exposed the lacy, frilly interior. It looked like a cross between a Stanley Steamer and an open casket.

I never pushed it—in or out of uniform. I agreed with our tough, old, battle-scarred top sergeant, a thirty-year veteran of three wars who had trained thousands of cadets to be shavetails. Day after day he had lined us up during officers' training and barked, "No self-respecting officer and gentleman will ever defile the uniform by pushing a baby carriage."

That chore, I agreed, should be left to my wife.

I felt even stronger when it came to umbrellas. Actually we've had a family taboo against umbrellas that goes back long before my days as an officer candidate.

My father, who had been an Army officer in World War I, never carried an umbrella. In fact—like liquor, playing cards and calendars with pictures of chesty women—we never had one in the house. We did have an umbrella stand in the front room, but it had belonged to my mother's father, Colonel Thompson (who wasn't a real colonel), and was only used to hold walking sticks and canes. When it rained, we "real men" got wet the way the good Lord intended.

But my reaction to the lecture in my military science class began to bother me. Our instructor, who stood ramrod straight with every hair of his burr haircut at attention, reminded us we were fighting men.

"Can you imagine," he sneered, "a thirteenth-century knight striding into battle carrying an umbrella?"

The entire class leaped to its feet and shouted in chorus: "NO, SIR!!"

But I had this nagging picture of myself out there in the rain, my armor soaking wet, rusting together at the joints. There I stood, helpless, while a dry, umbrella-carrying infidel ran his spear through one of my corroded joints. I knew then that I was not born to be a military man any more than I could remain a fundamentalist. I simply could not fit the mold of traditions.

Years later, as a Southern Baptist pastor, I found myself drifting from that hallowed military tradition, wondering if my anti-umbrella teachings were legitimate. After all, Ian Fleming's macho super-spy, James Bond— the ultimate in masculinity, the perfect combination of muscle and suave—carried an umbrella.

Old traditions die hard, however, and it took me a long time to adjust to my new resolve. At first I only carried an umbrella when I went out of town on one of my occasional trips to the Baptist headquarters in Nashville. But I was still a novice. Like a non-Pentecostal who has just discovered that the gifts of the Spirit are for today, I didn't know how to act. Having never carried an umbrella, I didn't know what to do with it when it wasn't raining. Do you swing it like a proper Britisher on his way to the House of Lords? And what should I do with it when I got to my destination? Hand it to the butler with my hat and gloves?

Only I didn't wear a hat. And the Baptist Sunday school board, contrary to rumor, didn't employ a butler. Worse, I was beginning to like the Dapper Dan image I was projecting. It's like carrying an expensive briefcase; when you carry a rolled-up umbrella, you ARE somebody.

Everything came into perspective one stormy March afternoon in Nashville, however. Before leaving home I realized I might come in contact with some denominational guru. If I projected the right image, he might invite me over to his kingdom to preach. When you're busy climbing the ecclesiastical ladder, getting to preach in a big church is very important. I went out and purchased a sixty-dollar Lord Ashley umbrella with a rosewood handle and stainless steel shank. It was imported from James E. Smith & Sons, the famous London shop on Knightsbridge Road that sells nothing but umbrellas and walking sticks. Just carrying it aboard the plane made me want to speak with a British accent.

That misty afternoon I emerged from the Baptist headquarters building and found myself standing on the rain-swept sidewalk beside the Southern Baptists' greatest legend: R.G. Lee, pastor of the huge Bellevue Baptist Church in Memphis. It was my chance to shine.

Stepping up to the curb beside the great preacher, I flicked off the safety catch on my sixty-dollar Lord Ashley. Clearing my throat to draw his attention, I popped it open.

Instantly the wind caught it. Before I could gulp, the Lord Ashley was inside out. Snatched from my hand by a mighty gust, it went flying into the middle of James Robertson Parkway in front of a Yellow Cab.

In one fleeting second it was smashed flat.

The great, old, silver-haired preacher—who legend said had preached his famous sermon "Pay Day, Some Day" over a thousand times—turned slowly and looked at me.

"When I was a young country preacher about your age," the great orator said in his cultured voice, "I once baptized a farmer in a fast-moving mountain stream. When he went under, I lost my grip. He resurfaced seventy-five yards downstream. His wife finally got hold of his leg and pulled him to shore, but the deacons had to roll him on a barrel to get the water out of him.''

As his taxi pulled up to the curb he looked kindly at me. ''Always open your umbrella the way you baptize—upstream. You'll lose a lot less that way.''

He entered the taxi and disappeared.

In the gutter across the street a beer truck could be heard crunching the remains of my sixty-dollar Lord Ashley into unrecognizable debris.

I've owned a lot of umbrellas since then. I've left most of them on airplanes or standing in the closets of Holiday Inns. But it's OK, because I've never again purchased one which cost more than ten dollars. And I always open them into the wind.

Old traditions do fade away, however. Last Sunday my brother, the Army general, visited our church. He was in full uniform since he had to catch a plane right after the service. When church dismissed we discovered it was pouring rain outside. Although he didn't hold it himself, he seemed highly pleased that I had an umbrella to cover us while we dashed to the car.

And yesterday after the church service I could be seen pushing a baby buggy—containing MY grandson.

Now, if only I could remember that third thing an officer and gentleman should never do, I could go out and break that tradition, too.

Let's Hear It for the Ghostwriters and Everyone Else Who Doesn't Care Who Gets the Credit

a fellow who comes to our church occasionally, a prophet-type, sent me some stuff in the mail. actually it was some insight he'd received on the resurrection of jesus. he thought it might help me while i was preparing my easter sermon. ''please don't give me any credit,'' he wrote. ''i just thought this might help you while you're preparing your sermon.''

i didn't agree with all his theology, but i sure agreed with his spirit. i mean, there aren't many folks around these days who don't want credit.

one of my childhood heroes was a cockroach named archy. actually, archy was a ghostwriter who slipped out of the woodwork at night and wrote stuff for his boss, poet don marquis. especially did he like to write saucy poems about mehitable the cat.

from his precarious perch on top of the typewriter carriage, archy would select the right key, then leap down headfirst, striking one slow letter after another.

true ghostwriters are always like that. committed. regardless of bloody foreheads and the fact someone else gets all the credit (and most of the money), they keep on, night after night, writing for the sake of getting the message out.

in archy's case, he was unable to strike the shift key to make capital letters. thus, even though *la cucaracha* seldom signed his name, his style became his signature. he was the e.e. cummings of the insect world, always writing in lower case.

ONE NIGHT ARCHY CLIMBED UP ON THE TYPEWRITER AND DISCOVERED, TO HIS UNBRIDLED JOY, THAT SOMEONE HAD LEFT THE SHIFT KEY DEPRESSED. THAT NIGHT, AS HE LEAPED FROM CARRIAGE TO KEY, HE WAS ABLE TO WRITE HIS MESSAGE IN BLAZING CAPITALS. FOR THE GHOST-WRITER, THAT IS THE DIFFERENCE BETWEEN WRITING A BOOK FOR BILLY GRAHAM AND SISTER NOBODY. SOMEONE ELSE STILL GETS THE CREDIT (AND THE MONEY), BUT, AH, THE JOY OF WRITING BIG.

everyone in a servant's role has at one time or another identified with archy. you bang your head against the wall—or your fingers against the keys—only to find someone else getting all the glory. that's the reason the letter from the part-time prophet in our church was such a blessing. he just wanted to make a contribution—the kind without any strings attached.

now it may come as a shock to a lot of gentle readers, but most famous christians don't write their books themselves. they hire an archy. sometimes they give them credit, like a little line on the cover that says "as told to," but most of the time they just take all the glory for themselves. oh, there are exceptions like catherine marshall, agnes sanford and norman grubb who wrote their own stuff. but when you read most of the others, pause for a moment and give silent tribute to the archys of the literary world—most of whom aren't even mentioned in the fine type of "credits" in the preface.

it's a lonely task. and sometimes the only compensation is a whisper in the night which says, "well done, arch. they get theirs now. i'm applying yours on a house just down the road from me."

i remember the pain i felt when my first book appeared. i had ghost-written it for nicky cruz—a really great guy—who had insisted my name go on the book jacket along with his. but when the book arrived in the mail i had to get a magnifying glass to find my name. even the name of billy graham who wrote the foreword was bigger than mine. (ironically, graham didn't write the foreword—his "ghost," an "archy" by the name of lee fisher, wrote it.) i complained to god and he reminded me that his name didn't appear on the dust jacket at all. well, that shamed me pretty good and i promised him i'd not complain again. in fact, i was willing to go totally unnoticed as long as he got first billing.

he took me at my word. my next book was entitled *god can do it again*. god and kathryn kuhlman made it in big letters on the dust jacket—and i was left off completely.

it took a while to work through all that ego garbage. but after being around a lot of strutting people and realizing how foolish i looked trying to strut in tennis shoes, i just decided that instead of being a ghostwriter i'd be a holy ghostwriter. that way, if anyone made fun of me because i couldn't spell or cheated me out of a royalty, i'd just turn them over to my daddy. (note: would you believe that of the fourteen publishers for whom I've written, the four i know who have cheated me on royalty payments have all gone bankrupt or been bought out.)

taking credit (or as god calls it, sharing the glory) is plumb foolish. one of the women i wrote for, a wonderful old dutch saint named corrie ten boom, once chastened me when i was complaining that i didn't get no respect. she said i reminded her of that palm sunday donkey, the one jesus rode into jerusalem while people threw palm branches in front of him. she asked me if i could imagine that donkey, swaggering with pride and nodding in feigned humility, thinking the people were shouting "hosannah" at him. she was too kind to say it, but i got her point: there's nothing worse than a proud jackass, unless it's some archy demanding credit.

several years ago we had a big men's meeting in the dining hall of the church. but no sooner had we finished with all the important introductions than there was an unbelievable racket in the kitchen. it sounded like a wild bull loose in the pantry. i rushed back and found—not a wild bull, but an angry archy. it was the church hostess, throwing pots and pans all over the place. she was upset that we hadn't brought her out and applauded her as we did the speaker of the evening.

"all i do is cook and clean," she screamed. "no one ever notices me."

well, we noticed her that night. i still remember it. but the question remains: if the archys are noticed, then how does god get the glory?

and if you think it's bad when the cook goes berserk at the men's meeting, you ought to be around some sunday morning when the organist gets mad, or the guy in the sound booth gets fed up because no one ever turns around and gives him a clap offering.

there are a lot of kingdom citizens assigned archy roles. ghostwriters. nursery workers. secretaries. instrumentalists. arrangers, composers, back-up musicians. editors. not to mention mechanics on the mission field and preachers' wives who babysit while their husbands do the strutting.

it takes a big person to live small.

one of the favorite stories around the publishing house is the time the author of the book *humility and how i attained it* spent the morning arguing with the publisher that his picture on the dust jacket wasn't big enough.

i guess the greatest miracle of all is that god loves us—even when we demand credit.

in the meantime, whenever you see a successful author, the leader of a worldwide ministry or a famous evangelist—don't get star-struck. most of them are just plain, dull, ordinary folks. but someplace, in the nocturnal areas of their lives—if you look deep enough—you'll find a servant. some hard-working cockroach pounding the keys with his head.

let's hear it for the archys of the kingdom.

My Name Is Not Pierre Cardin

Most of my life, it seems, has been spent paddling upstream. Others around me seem to be perfectly content drifting along with the current, yet here I am doggedly battling in the opposite direction.

Some of my friends say I am rebellious. Independent. Unsubmissive. Not so. I am simply determined to maintain my uniqueness, my individuality—those things which peer pressure seems dedicated to sweeping away.

I am weary, for instance, of being pushed around by fashion and advertising moguls who not only tell me what to wear but want to turn me into a walking billboard for their products.

It's bad enough that I have "Nike" and "Topsider" written on my favorite shoes. But what really steams me is to go into a store to buy a T-shirt and the only ones I can find have "Adidas" emblazoned on the chest. I don't mind penguins, little feet, a quartermaster's wheel, alligators, camels or even a leaf that looks strangely like a forbidden hallucinogenic plant. But I object when some shirt manufacturer wants me to become a signboard to advertise his name.

Last week my wife gave me a dress shirt that said Pierre Cardin on the pocket. Obviously she had me confused with an old boyfriend. Since my name is Jamie, not Pierre, I gave it back. Neither, by the way, is my name Levi, Hang Ten, Coca-Cola or Los Angeles Lakers.

I'm me.

Erma Bombeck tells about the time all the housewives in her neighborhood started wearing tennis clothes. She said at school one afternoon she passed a housewife in the hall who was headed for the office in full tennis attire.

"Excuse me," she said, "but the girls' rest room is out of paper towels."

"Why tell me?" the woman asked, nervously fingering her headband.

"You had 'HEAD' on your T-shirt, and I figured you were a restroom attendant."

The tough scene came at the auto dealer's when our new car arrived. It's bad enough wearing a "Rabbit" sign without being forced to be a rolling advertisement for Honest John's Auto Hutch.

Therefore, I asked Honest John to remove his little sign from the tailgate. When he showed dismay, I suggested a compromise. I would drive around with his little sign on my car if he would pay me a royalty of two cents per mile in the city and one cent per mile on the highway. That's the way songwriters do it, you know.

He didn't think that was funny—and removed the sign.

How would you like to show up at a swanky reception driving a car that had a sign "Fat Albert's Ford" on the trunk lid? When the parking valet asks which car is yours, you identify it by saying, "It has

'Bald Billy's Car Emporium' on the back.''

I had a bigger problem when it came to my wife's car. We bought it from a lady car dealer who calls herself "Big Momma." This time, since it was Jackie's car, I thought it would be appropriate to leave the sign on the trunk lid.

"Tell you what," Jackie said, "I'll drive the Rabbit with the little ears that look like the *Playboy* symbol and you can drive my car that says, 'I Shopped at Big Momma's.' ''

Big Momma just shrugged when I told her the sign had to go. "A lot of men used to like my sign," she said. "But I guess these scandals with the television evangelists have scared them off." Then she gave a big, dirty laugh and told the salesman to "hold the sign."

I'm not, as a friend accused, a cynic. But I am more than a piece of flotsam being washed along in the current.

I don't even care who makes my clothes as long as they fit and the zippers don't stick open in embarrassing situations. Jackie said she finally discovered who makes my shirts. After I finished preaching one Sunday she came up to the platform and began scratching on my shirt collar.

"What are you doing? This is a brand new shirt."

"That's what you get for getting dressed in the dark and not letting me inspect you before you left the house. I couldn't keep my mind on your sermon for looking at this piece of paper stuck on the side of your shirt collar. Every one in church was giggling at it."

"What piece of paper?"

By then she had scratched it off. "It's the name of the man who designed your shirt. His name is Inspector 54."

I never felt God had called me to unscrew my head and store my intellect in a jar; nor am I to put my brain in neutral and buzz with the swarm. I am one of a kind and therefore choose, as an act of my will, not to be lumped with the others.

I detest crowds. I stay home on July 4 and go to the beach when no one else is there so I can walk alone on the sand. The idea of being part of a crowd of one million people at a religious rally in Washington, D.C., horrifies me. I'd much rather be alone in the woods or sitting in a quiet restaurant with friends.

I value and protect my individuality—my uniqueness. It is the essence of being, the mark of creation, the reason for redemption. Christ did not die to make us robots but to restore us to personhood—even if my personhood is still a bit wild and crazy. ("Warped" is the word Jackie uses.)

I refuse to be labeled a "fundamentalist" or put in a "liberal" box. I describe myself as a "liberal conservative," although at times I call myself a "conservative liberal." One thing I am not is a "moderate," which conjures up the image of something that is neither hot nor cold and thus should be spewed.

I'm not a them—or a they. I'm a me.

The system tried to label Jesus, to give Him a title. That's the way the system controls you. Then you can be classified as a "they" or a "those." Jesus not only resisted titles, He resisted labels.

He, too, was a "me." Not a "they."

In other words, I can't imagine Jesus wearing a robe with a fancy little monogram stitched on the seat that said "Judah's."

Nor can I picture Him wearing a big gold cross around His neck.

I doubt if He wore a T-shirt under His robe that had "Jews for Jesus" silk-screened on the front or carried a copy of the Torah with "Maranatha" written on the leather cover.

I really can't see Him riding into Jerusalem on Palm Sunday with a saddle sticker on His donkey that said, "Bray if you love Jesus," or "In case of rapture this jackass will self-destruct."

He knew He was unique, but the purpose of His uniqueness was to point people to His Father—not to draw attention to Himself.

For years I refused to wear a necktie, simply because everyone else did. Then I began to hear things like "Jamie's one of *those* who never wears a tie."

That meant I had to go out and buy a bunch of neckties. The problem was most of them had the names of the French designers splashed all over the front.

But that's part of the price of swimming upstream. I would rather eat breakfast at Ethel and Fred's Place for $2.35, where everyone wears work clothes and sops up their sausage gravy with a biscuit, than have breakfast at Brennan's in New Orleans for $30. If time allows I drive the back roads rather than the interstates. I stay in small motels, wear old clothes and cut my own hair.

I choose not to wear a toupee, have never worn fingernail polish in my life, have decided I would never have my ears pierced, and would rather catch pneumonia than wear what my mother used to call "rubbers."

Can you imagine what it's like, having your mother let you out in front of the junior high school on a drizzly morning with all the big kids standing over to one side smoking and smirking, listening as she hollers out the car window, " 'Bye-bye, Sweetheart, be sure to wear your *rubbers* on the way home"?

It was about that time I decided I would be me. Just me.

Once when a tuxedo-wearing evangelist at a Full Gospel Business Men's convention announced that everyone in the room was going to be "slain in the Spirit" as he walked down the aisle, I was the only one who remained standing. My wife accused me (from her prone position under the chairs) of being stubborn, independent and rebellious.

I wasn't proud of my obstinacy. In fact, I was embarrassed. But since I have to live with myself, I choose not to play games—at least not with something as serious as that.

To surrender your individuality to the world is the worst of all blasphemies. Your uniqueness is your most precious possession. Don't waste it floating downstream.

Church Pecking Order

In the book *Help! I'm a Pastor's Wife*, my daughter-in-law Michele told of chatting with a couple of friends in a swanky little cafe outside Washington, D.C. She told them she was editing a book by and about pastors' wives. One of the gals remarked, "What's it about? How to throw the perfect tea party?"

I guess a lot of people think that's what pastors' wives do: play the piano at church and pour tea at the monthly social. In other words, they rank pretty low in kingdom pecking order.

I've not had much experience with pastors' wives. (My own wife sees to that.) But I have had a great deal of experience with pastors.

Most people suspect that, despite their diligent efforts to conceal it, pastors are people, too. Granted, a lot of them seem to go out of their way to convince us otherwise. But—if we dragged them out of their Cadillacs, took off their collars, snatched away their microphones and forbade them to use words like "brethren," "yonder" and "eschatology"—

we would discover they're just like the rest of us. Plain old people.

The reason most pastors look and act differently from just ordinary folks is they were taught—mostly by other pastors—that there is a certain pecking order in kingdom strata. Obviously, pastors who drive Cadillacs are higher in grade than pastors who drive pickup trucks. And the man who drives a BMW, or (sigh!) a Mercedes, ranks even higher. Ultimate status is achieved when the pastor and his wife drive color-matched Jaguars. In the words of Sambo, he's the "grandest tiger in all the jungle"—especially if he polishes his fingernails.

Kingdom ranking has been around since James and John vied for the right-hand seat beside Jesus in heaven. Today, however, the ranking is much more complicated, given all the offices and strata in the church. In order to define today's hierarchy I have devised a scale which explains the power structure. It's called the Accepted Liturgical Scale (ALS) and is graded on a scale of one (least) to twelve (greatest).

1. *Pastor's wife.* (However, if she drives her own Cadillac, she ranks equal to district superintendent.)

2. *Plain old ordinary pew-sitting, hymn-singing, money-giving, hard-working church member.*

3. *Sunday school teacher.* You have to be careful here, for there are ranks inside the Sunday school teacher category. a. *Nursery workers* are at the bottom. b. *Youth workers* are next to the bottom because they never seem to last very long and most of them wind up fleeing into the desert where they rip their clothes and beat their heads on rocks. c. *Adult teachers* are at the top, but their ranking also depends on how large a class they teach and how wealthy and famous their class members are. (For instance, a class which contains the mayor, an assistant to the governor or a wealthy widow ranks higher than a class of Yuppies or dump truck drivers.)

4. *Church staff member.* All staff members except church secretaries are included on this level. The church secretary is rated at 1.5. In other words, she can snub the pastor's wife but is treated like dirt by everyone else. However, in churches of more than 3,000 members, the pastor's personal secretary is rated equal with archbishop.

5. *Pastor.*

6. *Missionary.* While I prefer to rank missionaries number twelve, some Christians don't even recognize them as people, rating them lower

than pastor's wife. I've given them a number six to please both camps.

7. *Priest.* All kinds, even those who drink beverages with little olives and onions in the bottom of the glass. Actually, priests should be ranked on the same level as pastors, but because they wear funny clothes and act mysteriously I had no choice but to put them in the number seven slot.

8. *Traveling teacher.* (Traveling teachers who don't get invited to big conferences are rated at the number four level.) This category includes:

a. *Catholic theologians.*

b. *Evangelists/40,000 minimum crusade audience.* (Tent evangelists are ranked with dump truck drivers.)

c. *Christian psychologists.*

d. *Christian publishers.* This only includes publishers who sell their stuff. Publishers who give their literature away to the poor or the stingy are ranked in the same category with youth directors. Nor does it apply to book editors, especially those who have soupstains all over their neckties. These sloppy and pathetic people deserve no higher rank than plain old church members. Some of them—if we're honest about it—should be rated in the same category as pastor's wife.

e. *Seminary professors.* (Unless they teach religious education or music, which drops them down to number three.)

f. *Traveling musicians.* (Note: Frankly, rock musicians should not be ranked at all, but because of the kind of cars they drive and their flashy wardrobe, popular opinion forces inclusion.)

9. *College president.* Chancellors (Pat Robertson variety) are included if they live in mansions on the edge of the campus.

10. *Bishop and television personalities.*

11. *Archbishop.*

12. *Pope John Paul and Billy Graham.* Some Pentecostal groups may substitute "general superintendent." Nearly all TV evangelists put themselves at this level.

Now comes Michele's book which does something extremely important. It proves the ALS ratings are upside down. The least in the kingdom is really the greatest. No one deserves higher honor than the pastor's wife. I know. I married one.

Please Close Your Heads

Well, it finally happened.

I was on the platform during the early service that Sunday morning. Although we had a guest preacher, I was directing the service. Our church soloist, Jimmy Smith, was singing from the piano. It was powerful, moving: *"I will pour water on him that is thirsty...."*

As he finished, I turned to the guest preacher, who was seated beside me. "I'm going to lead in prayer before you preach," I whispered.

He nodded. I picked up the wireless microphone and walked to the pulpit just as the music finished.

"Please bow your heads and close your eyes," I said. Jimmy caught the mood and continued to play softly. I talked for a moment about the water of the Holy Spirit which softens the parched earth of our lives. I asked the people to let Him come into their lives. Jimmy sang another stanza. Some of the people slipped to their knees. I closed by asking them to receive the seed of the Word which the preacher was about to sow in their lives.

It was good stuff. Even I was amazed at how good God can do it when I get out of the way.

After the service the guest preacher commented, "That was great. I wish you could repeat it just the same way at the second service."

I swelled a little. It *was* a good word. Fresh. Spontaneous. I nodded. If a thing is good for one group, why not for all?

In the second service, before a much larger crowd, Jimmy sang the same song. But something was different. The people were not responding as the first group had. But my course was set. Once again I picked up the microphone and stepped to the pulpit. With solemn drama I called the people to prayer.

My own eyes were closed. My head bowed. I waited, piously, through the dramatic pause. Instead of the expected silence, however, I heard laughter. It started in the side section where my wife and grown children were sitting. It rippled across the congregation, like dry leaves before the wind, growing louder and louder.

I stood there, puffed-up and dumb, wondering what was happening. Was something going on that was funny and I couldn't see it because my eyes were closed?

I opened my eyes and immediately squeezed them shut. The people were laughing so hard they were crying. Then, in that horrifying way a person knows, I knew. They were laughing at me. Surely it wasn't my zipper?

Only then did I recall what I had just said. It ran through my thoughts like a tape replay. I had said, *"Please bow your eyes and close your heads."*

I love it when it happens to other stuffed shirts. Now it was my turn.

Memories, like rabbits in front of hounds, raced wildly across my mind.

I remembered the time I came to the platform to officiate in a formal wedding. I had just come out of the bathroom and didn't realize until I was in front of all those people that stuck to my shoe and trailing behind was an eight-foot stream of toilet paper.

I remembered the time I looked down in the middle of my sermon and saw my pants were unzipped—and my shirt tail was sticking out like a flag.

I remembered the time I put my hand on a casket at the front of the church and the flimsy stand it was sitting on gave way.

Then I remembered that Easter morning baptismal service some years ago. The baptistry was high above the choir loft. My plan was to baptize at the beginning of the service then rush to the platform during the hymn so I could preach. That morning I wore my new waders—huge rubber boots which came up to my chest, held in place by suspenders. The last person to be baptized was an ample woman. I mean "ample" as in "enormous." When I lowered her beneath the surface she displaced far more water than I anticipated. The overflow rushed into my waders, filling them to the brim. When the woman came up, the water went down—leaving me standing in 400 pounds of water-filled boots. I was rooted to the bottom of the baptistry and couldn't move. I finally had to lower my suspenders and crawl out of the boots in front of the entire Easter congregation—in my underwear.

The very next week—seven days too late—the ladies' missionary society installed a draw curtain in the baptistry.

All that ran through my mind and I realized, "I've been here before."

I knew if I tried to correct my mistake it would get worse. But what do you do? The one thing I didn't want to do was laugh. I wanted to be like Elijah and suddenly disappear in a whirlwind, never to be seen again. But the more I thought of what had just happened, the funnier it seemed. Here's a solemn, pious, stuffed shirt who comes strutting to the pulpit with ministerial pomp and, accompanied by soft music, intones, "PLEASE BOW YOUR EYES AND CLOSE YOUR HEADS!"

I began to giggle. The congregation howled. They were now laughing so hard people were holding their stomachs.

Gradually I realized what had happened. What God had done in the early service I had tried to duplicate in my own strength. God, who enjoys a good laugh too, figured since I was going to take the credit, He might as well let me do it my way. My way, always, is to stick my foot in my mouth.

When you want the people to notice you, God usually says, "Be My guest!" But what they remember is often something you wish they'd forget.

I twice tried to salvage the moment, but it was too far gone. The best I could do was walk over to the preacher, who was sitting there shaking his head, and say, "You're on."

The preacher did his best that morning, but he would have been far more effective had he just said the benediction. The sermon had already been preached by the dumbbell who tried to upstage God.

It doesn't pay to take yourself seriously when God is present.

Mirror, Mirror, on the Wall, Who's the Fairest of Them All?

Every year for the last several years I have received a letter asking me to nominate my choice for the "Christian Woman of the Year." One year's letter contained a nomination ballot saying my vote "along with other key evangelical leaders will help the executive committee determine the will of God."

Since I wanted to be helpful—especially in assisting executive committees determine the will of God—and since I loved being listed as a "key evangelical leader," I decided to cooperate.

The committee itself was impressive. It included:

• Carolyn Evans, wife of evangelist Mike Evans;

• Mary Crowley, millionaire Dallas businesswoman who has an

entire building in Dallas's First Baptist Church named for her (who has since gone on to glory where she has doubtlessly revised her concepts of "greatness");

• Anne Murchison, wife of the former owner of the Dallas Cowboys;

• Dede Robertson, wife of televangelist Pat Robertson, who was destined to become the nation's first lady until a funny thing happened on Super Tuesday;

• Dr. Cory Ser Vaas, publisher of the *Saturday Evening Post*;

• Karen Davis, whose husband, a Texas millionaire, almost went to prison when accused of murdering his first wife.

The letter asked me to vote for one of seven women on the ballot. This would help the committee "honor a woman who has given outstanding service in the ministry and who has led an exemplary Christian life."

The ballot then listed the ladies-in-waiting—a virtual Who's Who in the kingdom:

• political activist Beverly LaHaye;

• Dee Jepsen, wife of a former congressman;

• Frances Swaggart, wife of a now-defrocked televangelist (this was before her husband lost his frock);

• evangelist and pastor's wife Anne Gimenez;

• Evelyn Roberts, wife of Oral;

• Vonette Bright, wife of campus crusader Bill Bright;

• Bible teacher Marilyn Hickey (whose husband wears a wig which sometimes falls off and floats in the water scaring people to death).

Mirror, mirror, on the wall, who's the fairest of them all? Who was I, a mere man, to make a selection from this lineup? I knew them all. Unlike most lists of the rich and famous, I didn't know a single disqualifying thing about any of them. All were worthy of honor.

The year before, the committee had selected Mrs. Billy Graham as first lady in the kingdom. But who was to wear the crown this year? Was Marilyn Hickey more worthy of honor than Bill Bright's wife? Maybe I should vote for Anne Gimenez—after all, she had to live with my friend John. But then look how long Evelyn had put up with Oral. And what of poor Frances Swaggart?

Even though there wasn't a line for "other," I considered nominating my ninety-year-old mother. If anyone in the world was worthy of honor it was she. But to list her meant I would be classifying myself with all those other biggies in the kingdom. After all, I was her son. I wasn't sure how I could get away with it. Maybe if I mailed my ballot from Boston no one would know it came from me.

Then there was another factor. Would my nomination really count? What if this was just a political ploy? You know, someone's little scheme to get "in" with the "movers and shakers." The way to be honored, you know, is to pass out honors. That's the reason people give expensive gifts to kings—in hopes the king will honor them in return. Could it be that Mike Evans...?

I shook the thought from my head. Surely not! After all, the letter did say the committee would prayerfully consider each nomination. Yes, I would nominate my mother.

I leaned back in my chair and imagined what it would be like. I pictured this wonderful committee, sitting around Carolyn Evans' breakfast table in Ft. Worth. They had spent most of the morning in prayer. Mary Crowley had flown in the night before in her custom-designed DC-9 to be there for the opening of the ballots. Dr. Ser Vaas opened the meeting with a little devotional about the value of eating high-fiber food to keep the lower bowel free of cancer-causing debris. She then passed out samples of L-lysine. Anne Murchison led in prayer, asking God to give wisdom to the committee and to take the Cowboys all the way to the Super Bowl.

There was a gentle knock at the kitchen door. Mike Evans had arrived. Carolyn took a key from her pocketbook and unlocked the handcuff which fastened the mailbag to her husband's left wrist. Mike emptied the ballots on the table. There were, just as my invitation letter stated, "more than 300 ballots submitted by the most influential evangelical leaders of America."

Carolyn divided the letters into equal stacks. The six ladies began their solemn task—opening envelopes, calling out names, marking them down. Two votes for Marilyn. Three votes for Beverly. Five votes for Evelyn (all in an ORU envelope).

Then one of the committee members, say Dede Robertson, came to my envelope. I could see her lips moving in silent prayer (remember, the invitation letter promised the committee would prayerfully consider each nominee) as she slipped the letter opener under the flap. She was praying in the Spirit, asking God to speak to her through the enclosed ballot.

"One write-in vote for ninety-year-old Elvira Buckingham," she stated, trying to keep the excitement out of her voice. "She's the widow of Walter Buckingham and lives on Social Security in a retirement home in Florida."

The other committee members looked up. Eyes round. Lips quivering. Dede was holding the ballot out for everyone to see. Her hands were trembling. Tears were running down the faces of two of the ladies.

Dr. Ser Vaas spoke, her voice choked with emotion. "How could we have missed her in the original nominations?"

"Oh, God, forgive us," Karen Davis wept.

"I don't think we need go any further," the chairperson said in a quivering voice. The rest agreed.

No, I said to myself, shaking myself out of my reverie. It won't work. Even if they nominated my mother, she wouldn't accept. In the first place she wouldn't be willing to fly to Washington to receive the award since she feels that money spent on plane tickets for awards banquets would be much better spent if given to missions. She doesn't even have a television set. When we gave her one she made us take it back and give her the money instead. Then she took the money and sent it to a missionary in Indonesia. You see, she believes it's a sin for her to hear the gospel twice when most people in the world haven't heard it at all. Not only that, she's the only person I know who doesn't have an opinion on Jimmy Swaggart. In fact, since she doesn't have a TV set, she doesn't even know who Jimmy Swaggart is. Besides that, she's committed herself to staying home and praying four hours a day for various missionaries. A trip to receive the "Christian Woman of the Year" award would interrupt that.

In the end I wound up nominating my wife, who lives with a mission field. Me.

Two weeks later I received a notice from the committee: "Please submit a serious ballot." I wrote back, saying I was serious. I doubted if any of those on the formal ballot lived with as much adversity as Jackie.

A month later I received a mailgram. Beverly LaHaye had been named "Christian Woman of the Year." The president and seventy-five senators and congressmen sent wires of congratulations. I spent the afternoon taking my mother for a drive and thinking of something Jesus said:

"I tell you the truth, this poor widow has put in more than all the others."

Barley Brown

For years my wife has drunk something called Barley Green. Every morning, while I'm fixing my coffee, I hear her across the kitchen mixing this green powder with cranberry juice, then gagging and coughing as she swallows it.

"If you'd drink this you'd live longer. It resupplies all the vitamins you leech out of your system by drinking that coffee."

I tried it several times and concluded it was better to risk a vitaminless life than to start the day gagging and retching.

We have a nutritional expert in our church who insists this elixir has wonderful medicinal and restorative qualities. It cleans out your cells, restores your blood and fills you with vitamins and minerals. It's as though the Fountain of Youth has been freeze-dried and put in a jar.

Unfortunately, it has the consistency and taste of dried cow's cud. As a cow eats tender barley shoots for her afternoon siesta snack, belches it back up in big green globs and lies contentedly in the pasture chewing her regurgitation—so with Barley Green. Only instead of going through a cow's innards, it is processed in a biology laboratory.

Unlike cow's cud, however, Barley Green is not free. Instead it is sold by Christians—several of whom are in our church.

That's the reason I'm now promoting Barley Brown, which is absolutely free and is much better for you. Barley Green is expensive and has only been regurgitated once. Barley Brown has been totally processed. All you need is a cow, or access to a neighbor's pasture. Since we have four cows we have an almost unlimited supply of Barley Brown. Once its dried and powdered you mix it with milk (another "totally processed" cow's product) and it makes a delicious brown drink. If you pretend it's chocolate you'll not gag. It's really caught on in our church. Our youth have packaged and sold enough (they call it "the product") to finance a summer mission to Waikiki, supposedly to witness to surfers on the beach.

The problem is now everyone is selling it. What do you say when a Barley Brown agent wants to teach a Sunday school class on nutrition—

and you know he's going to wind up taking orders?

We went through this with Amway. Dozens of our people attended the big Amway conventions. They returned to our church with glazed eyes, their chests covered with "I Can Do It!" buttons and satchels full of everything from sink cleaner to shoe polish. I still recall seeing one of our elders, assigned to stand at the church door and shake hands during January, handing out Amway order forms while his wife was on her knees spraying shoe polish on the men's shoes. Gasp!

Then it was Shaklee vitamins. At one time we had thirty-one Shaklee distributors in our church—each one wanting to give a Sunday morning testimony. The biggest problem came at the altar rail. One morning I overheard a Shaklee distributor prophesying to a man with one leg, "Thus saith the Lord who heals the halt and the lame, buy Shaklee from my servant."

Double gasp!

Herbalife was almost as bad. Choir members showed up wearing huge buttons saying, "Ask me about Herbalife." It was easy to spot the fellow who was selling Herbal Laxative. He always had to get up at least twice during the service to rush to the bathroom. He really didn't need his "Be a Regular Fellow!" button. He was his own greatest advertisement on the effectiveness of his product.

Besides Barley Brown, the only vitamins I take are pills made from dried seaweed and marine algae sold by a former program director at PTL. They turn your urine bright green—which causes amazing reactions when I use the public rest room at an airport.

The problem is not the products. I can testify to the effectiveness of each. (Warning to preachers: do not take Herbal Laxative before you preach.) The problem is, What do you do when your church is filled with wonderful people all selling competitive wonderful products? My wife said she finally discovered why Pentecostal Holiness women don't wear makeup. It has nothing to do with holiness. It's their only defense against the problems caused by choosing Vanda over Avon and Mary Kay—all sold by the wives of influential deacons.

I faced this several years ago when all three candidates for the county sheriff's race showed up in church on the same Sunday morning. All three had relatives in the church who were handing out leaflets. The incumbent, whose wife was pastor of the local spiritualist church, came in uniform. One of the candidates, who had been in local politics a long time and knew the ropes, came to the altar for prayer—shaking hands all the way down and back up the aisle. The other fellow—who had a brace on one leg, thus qualifying for a disabled parking permit— parked his big van, covered with "Vote for Me" signs, right in front of the building. It was the huge speakers on top playing "The Stars and Stripes Forever" that caused the fistfights after the service, though. His van remained three days since the incumbent's nephew let the air out of all his tires.

And that's why the only product I endorse from the pulpit is Barley Brown—guaranteed to make you grow spiritually.

FIVE

Living Thin Off the Fat of the Land

Every day for the first fifty years of my life I was fat. When I was born my Aunt Beulah, who was helping as midwife, took one look at me and said, "Now there's a fat baby!" I weighed in at twenty-five percent above normal and continued to grow proportionately until, at age fifty, I could only be described as a blubbery, fat hulk.

All those years I was a slave to things like strawberry shortcakes, biscuits and jelly, mashed potatoes and coconut cream pies. Normal people, I understood, could eat one biscuit, one piece of pie, one scoop of ice cream. Me, I could inhale the entire contents of a refrigerator.

Get angry and I'd eat a half-gallon of ice cream.

Get nervous and I'd eat an entire apple pie.

When it was time to celebrate—like when I finished a manuscript and put it in the mail—I'd go out and eat four hot dogs, complete with chips and two scoops of cottage cheese on the side. Then, by the time I got home I'd be so thirsty I'd drink a full two-liter bottle of soda pop. (None of that diet stuff, it gives you cancer.)

It was a big mistake when I installed a twelve-foot extension cord on the kitchen phone so Jackie could walk around the kitchen while talking on the phone. It also meant I could get to the chocolate pudding in the refrigerator while talking to an angry church official. If he was angry enough, I would consume seven or eight of those little dessert dishes filled with pudding that Jackie had put in the refrigerator to cool before dinner.

While some people have their problems with alcohol and others with drugs, my problem came the moment I stepped into the cafeteria line at Morrison's and saw all those desserts. How could anyone, I wondered, eat just one?

And why did they always put them first in the cafeteria line? If they were last, where desserts ought to be, I wouldn't be so tempted—having by then filled my tray with other stuff. Yet, if they were last, everyone else would probably feel the same way.

There had been times when, unable to find any pie, ice cream or tapioca pudding in the refrigerator, I would grab a spoon and eat an entire container of Cool Whip—justifying it on the basis that each tablespoon contained only sixteen calories. (That is, if the tablespoon is *level* full.) One time, in a hunger frenzy, I ate two dozen fresh chocolate chip cookies—but not before spreading them with margarine. Sometimes I'd spread grape jelly on them, and on other occasions I'd dip them in the Cool Whip and use them as eatable spoons.

If Jackie were planning to cook a macaroni casserole, she knew to buy twice the amount of cheddar cheese, for sooner or later I'd find it in the refrigerator. I could easily consume a pound of cheese without blinking. I liked it best when I sliced it thin and poured huge amounts of catsup on each slice. Thin slices, I lied to myself, were less fattening than just pulling back the plastic wrap and biting off a huge hunk like a grizzly bear chewing salmon.

What was true of pie, ice cream, biscuits, puddings and cheese was even truer when it came to doughnuts, and especially to glazed apple fritters. Doughnuts, one of my fat friends once told me, were less fattening if you only ate half of one at a time. Or if you waited until they were a day old and didn't taste very good. But I found I could consume twenty-four halves in the same amount of time it took me to consume a dozen full doughnuts—about ten minutes.

Resolutions to stop eating did no more than stir up the gluttony demon which had been my constant companion since I drew my first hungry suck of milk from my mother. I described myself as "stocky," but truthfully, I was fat. Blubbery fat. I did everything I knew to get it off. Nothing worked.

A number of my friends, knowing my struggles, advised I go on a diet. The problem was each of them had tried at least nine different diets, and all were as fat as I.

I only knew two people who had lost significant amounts of weight. One was a book editor who was now twice the size I was. The other was a lady evangelist who took it off, wrote a book and put it back on—with extras. I justified my fat by saying I'd rather stay fat than lose it and put it back on like my friends had done.

Jackie agreed to help me, however, and one Monday I came down to breakfast to be presented with something called the grapefruit diet. I lost twenty pounds in the first two weeks, but my blood pressure went up forty notches and I shouted at my wife, slammed doors behind the children and kicked the dog. On top of that I prowled the house at night, like an alcoholic looking for a hidden bottle of wine under the sofa cushions. Only I was looking for cookies, cheese and candy bars.

One night, a week after I started on the diet, I opened a drawer and right before my eyes was a Hershey bar. I glanced around, realized nobody had seen me, and quickly closed the drawer—my mouth watering. I knew it belonged to somebody. Hershey bars don't just appear in the drawer with the scissors, Christmas candles and 300 mismatched Uno cards. No, someone was hiding it there for a special purpose. But I had found it, and now it was mine. I planned to come down after dark and eat it up.

But I couldn't wait that long. An hour later, while the children were out in the yard playing, I returned.

The candy bar was gone! Frantically, I sorted through the Christmas candles and looked under all those Uno cards. Nothing. It was gone! I slammed the drawer shut at more than 100 miles an hour, catching the tip of my left index finger in the crack. While I was too big to cry over lost candy, I was not too big to cry over a smashed fingernail. I went outside, sat on the steps and sucked my finger.

The next afternoon I was prowling, looking for stashed candy from last Halloween's trick-or-treat. I knew the kids sometimes hid that stuff in their closets and drawers and forgot about it. It was then I found the Hershey bar wrapper in my daughter's bedroom trash can. I felt bad, knowing I had almost eaten what she had probably bought with her allowance and hidden from her gluttonous brothers. In fact, I felt so bad I went downstairs and ate half a jar of peanut butter.

The outcome of that particular diet was a gain of eight pounds, backing up the statement of my physician brother who says: "A diet is a torturous period of doing without food that precedes an increase of weight."

"What do you suggest?" I asked him in desperation.

"Are you eating food?" he asked.

"Yes."

"Well, give it up—especially any food that tastes good. If you crave a sandwich, make one without bread."

"Without bread?"

"Two pieces of lettuce with some raw spinach inside."

I took up jogging. If you jog in the afternoon you're subject to neighborhood ridicule, so I tried jogging in the early morning. The first morning out I was chased by a huge, brown dog with bloodshot eyes and toenails that went "clickety-click" on the concrete behind me. I sprinted two miles through the subdivision, losing four pounds. However, what I gained physically, I lost emotionally and was unable to speak clearly for five days. In fact, even today whenever I see a large, brown dog with bloodshot eyes, I pant.

The next time I went out was under cover of night. Jogging down a back alley, I paused to gulp some air and heard a terrifying scream from a nearby house.

"There he is, Howard. I told you he'd come back and try it again!" I heard a back screen door slam and what sounded distinctly like somebody cocking a shotgun. It was windsprints home again, accompanied by a ripped-up sweatsuit and long scratches on the inside of my thigh from vaulting a chain-link fence that almost cost me far more than skin.

"Your brother, who is five years older than you, does 100 push-ups each morning,'' my mother reminded me. Well, I'd had to fight his specter all my life, so I bought the Royal Canadian Air Force book of calisthenics and got to work.

The first morning, grunting and sweating in my pajamas, I jumped and bounced between the bed and the chest of drawers. I heard a squeal behind me and turned to see one of my teenage daughters with her hand over her mouth.

"It bounces just like jelly, Daddy,'' Bonnie giggled. That sent me into the kitchen where I found a bag of week-old doughnuts to ease the embarrassment.

I consulted my friend, Harvey Hester, who is a psychotherapist. Other than the fact that he was definitely neurotic, had a sick sense of humor and was fatter than I, I felt I could trust him. He suggested a test I could perform to determine whether I really needed to lose weight or not.

"A lot of fat people are actually in marvelous shape,'' he said, mentioning Russian weightlifters and those big Japanese wrestlers who wear diapers. He said I should strip off all my clothes and lie down flat on the floor. Then I should push myself up into a headstand. He said if I had problems with this, I should get Jackie to hold my feet to steady me. If she broke out into gales of laughter I should ignore it and continue the exercise. (Statistics prove that very few wives are capable of holding the feet of their naked husbands, while they are standing on their heads, without giggling.) The other thing he told me to watch out for would be her tendency to tickle me behind the knees. In fact it would be best if I could learn to stand on my head unassisted.

The purpose of this, he said, was to test my physical responses. Temporary deafness and nausea were to be expected. These are merely symptoms of middle age. The thing I should check for, he pointed out, was blindness.

"If everything goes dark and you have trouble breathing, you have a serious problem,'' he said seriously. "It means your fat has slipped down and covered your head.''

He then broke into hilarious laughter and staggered out of his office clutching his sides, repeating his sick joke to all the people waiting in his front office. Most of them laughed so hard they got healed and didn't have to keep their appointments, meaning he lost hundreds of dollars for which I was glad.

Nothing worked. I was doomed to being fat. I knew the issue was critical when the clothing store clerk snickered in my face when I said I wore a size thirty-eight skivvy.

Another clerk even had the audacity to say, "Sir, if you'll stop holding your breath I can get a correct measurement."

For years I had watched my fat friends lose weight, then condemn the rest of us fatties for not being spiritual. The most obnoxious person in the world is the man who has just stopped smoking; the second most obnoxious is the fellow who has just lost thirty pounds.

A couple of years ago the bookstores were glutted (appropriate word) with books on how to lose weight. Unfortunately, many of the people who wrote those books—like my two friends—are now fat again.

Several years ago I lost fifteen pounds on a fast. I immediately went into the pulpit and "called the body to slimness."

A lot of fat people left the church.

Not to be outdone, I wrote a magazine column on the subject. The art director, greatly inspired, illustrated the article with the picture of a specially designed suit of armor for fat people. The caption under this deformed monstrosity read: "Put on the whole armor of God."

That really stirred things up. The magazine got scores of letters from folks saying I was making fun of pregnant women and people with glandular problems.

Even though I had just written a little book called *Coping With Criticism* in which not a single cope said to go out and eat ice cream, I reacted to the nasty letters by going out and eating ice cream—twenty-five pounds' worth.

Yet with all my huffing and puffing when I climbed stairs, and my bulging eyeballs every time I bent over to tie my shoes, I knew there was something inherently sinful about being overweight. The idea of a fat Jesus, his pecs layering down over a fifty-five-gallon stomach, didn't fit even my radical concept of the Son of God. Besides, being fat in a world that is starving to death just seemed to be plain hypocritical.

Yet nothing—no amount of dieting or fasting—seemed to change my shape or weight. "Your body should be the temple of the Holy Spirit," I preached one day to a group of young people in a big tent at a Jesus rally.

My well-muscled friend Larry Tomczak, who has a body like Adonis, came up to me after I finished and whispered: "Your body isn't the temple of the Holy Spirit—it's a cathedral."

He was right, and all I could do was waddle away, looking for a hot dog stand to ease the pain.

"Inside every fat man is a thin man trying to get out," Woody Allen once quipped. However, there was room in me for an entire army of thin men.

One spring our home church (all of whom were overweight and some of whom were just plain fat) decided it was time to get in shape. We began bringing a set of bathroom scales to our Monday night meetings and weighing in. We fined ourselves significant amounts of money for each pound gained. One night, when we went out to eat as a group, we even took the scales to the Chinese restaurant.

It was all a big joke and by the end of the allotted period I was not only fatter, I was poorer. I was doomed unless God worked a miracle.

Miracles, I discovered, are often withheld until a man gets serious with himself—and with God. My miracle began the morning before my fiftieth birthday. I hated turning fifty. While fifty is a great number for the states in the Union or the speed limit, I dreaded being described as a fifty-year-old man. Only yesterday I was in high school. Back then old people were forty and were, as Bill Cosby used to say, always looking for a place to sit down. Fifty-year-olds were people getting ready to die—of old age.

That morning I was standing in the shower feeling sorry for myself. It was bad enough that I had become a grandfather. Now the second worst thing that could happen was about to take place. I was going to become fifty and shortly after that I would die.

Standing there, with the water running down my body, God said, "If you'll stop grumbling I'll give you some good news."

"I desperately need some good news."

"I'll let you live to be 100 if you'll cooperate with Me."

"God, I'm in a mess. I don't want to die young, but I don't want to be 100, either. What could be worse than to lie around a nursing home like a fat turnip?"

"That's not what I had in mind. I'll give you another fifty years of productive and creative life. All you have to do is cooperate with Me."

That was all He said. When I asked Him what He meant by

"cooperating," He stopped talking. I turned off the water and stepped out of the shower to dry off. Glancing up into the bathroom mirror I suddenly knew what God was talking about. My face was puffy. Jowly was a better word. My eyelids drooped. I needed a brassiere, and my tummy was so big I couldn't see my feet, much less my knees or any other important parts of my anatomy below my chest.

I wasn't dying; I was being crushed to death.

I was a pitiful sight, standing there like a flesh-colored watermelon. "I will not bring on you any of the diseases I brought on the Egyptians, for I am the Lord who heals you," God had told the Israelites at the springs of Marah. But that promise, like all God's promises, was in the subjunctive mood. It did not apply to the self-indulgent: those who ate six butter-soaked waffles for breakfast and three strawberry shortcakes before going to bed. All that did was bring on the plagues of Egypt.

Later that day I spent time examining all my false starts toward slimness. My failures, it seemed, stemmed from wrong motives. I wanted to look good, wanted to brag to fat folks, wanted people to envy me, wanted to impress women, wanted to strut—all insufficient. The one thing I didn't find on my list was wanting to lose weight to please God. No wonder I was still fat.

It took me another two months before I got desperate enough to please God. During that time my weight soared like a runaway balloon. I was doing everything possible to displease, not please, God.

The morning of June 1, I waddled down the stairs and put a chart on the door of my refrigerator. I ran a line from my weight that morning of 225 to my goal of 170. I'll not bore you with the details, for when you finally mean business with God one diet is as good as another.

The result was a weight loss of fifty-five pounds in ninety days.

During that time I totally changed my eating habits—and my wardrobe. When I reached my goal I literally burned my britches behind me. I could never return to the land of fat; it would cost me a fortune just to start over again in clothes.

One Sunday morning, six months later, I showed up in church carrying a clear plastic garbage bag filled with fifty-five pounds of beef fat from a local butcher's shop. I showed the people my bag of fat then preached from Hebrews 12:1—*"Let us lay aside every weight and the sin which doth so easily beset us.''* A bunch of fat folks got angry and left the church. They said just because I heard God in the shower didn't mean everybody had to. They said that God loves fatties, too.

I agree, but it was just too good an object lesson to pass up.

SIX

Should Vacations Be Outlawed?

Coming Apart

I'm swearing off vacations. They're just not worth it. It takes a week to get ready, two weeks to recover and six months to pay for them.

One summer while the kids were small we decided to combine our family vacations with my speaking tours. The first one was up the east coast of Florida. That wasn't so bad. We failed to take into account, however, that showing up at a swanky hotel with five children when the sponsoring church had only reserved one bed (and only agreed to pay for one bed) could cause a great deal of embarrassment in the lobby. Gratefully, that only happened three nights in a row, then we headed back home. That portion of the vacation cost us $700 and lost us friends in three cities who, although they smiled sweetly when our army finally left town, gave the distinct impression we'd never hear from them again.

The second "vacation" was a little better planned. We drove from Florida to Oklahoma, Missouri and Kansas where I had enough sense to warn people ahead of time how many were traveling with me. Since it is a known fact that anyone who travels to Kansas in July has a severe maladjustment of the mind, the fact I was bringing five children, an angry wife and a pregnant cat with me did not seem to upset my hosts. They had rightly figured that anyone who accepted their invitation would be what Colonel Thompson used to call "daft in the head."

Now I am thoroughly convinced they were right. Five thousand miles of motels and five children crowded into a station wagon with enough clothes to last two weeks and expecting the cat to give birth at any minute is ample evidence of a man's insanity. Besides that, each night I was facing a ballroom full of expectant people waiting for me to impart gems of spiritual wisdom.

The final phase of our three-part family vacation found us leaving to spend four days in eastern North Carolina. I was to speak Thursday, Friday, Saturday and Sunday in different cities—plus do a television interview in Raleigh and one of those abominable book-autographing parties on a sidewalk in Moorehead City on Saturday afternoon arranged by another writer, Irene Burk Harrell, who delights in making competitive authors suffer.

Our primary obstacle was just getting out of town. We had hoped to be on our way by 2 p.m. but by 5:30 it was apparent we were going to be a bit late. It was one of those afternoons when everything nailed down came loose. The telephone rang constantly. The house down the street caught fire and our yard was full of fire trucks and about 200 gawkers from the neighborhood. Our missionary friends with their six children who were spending the night told us not to worry, that they would close up when they left early in the morning; and the girl from the church called to say that two of my old alcoholic buddies had just walked in at the same time—both drunk.

On top of this, I realized I had not written my magazine column, which meant if I didn't make deadline a lot of people would be mad, mad, mad. I had no choice but to rush back in the house and sit at my typewriter while the five children, angry wife, and cat (now with five kittens) sweltered in the car. It was this last item which sent my wife into a screaming delirium, accompanied by slamming doors and threats to pull the phone out of the wall and throw it all the way to Altamonte Springs where the magazine has its editorial offices—seventy-five miles away.

I finished the column, and just as I rushed out of the house I heard a terrible racket in the utility room—evidence that the bearings in the air conditioner had given way and the entire unit was tearing up.

I hesitated and started back in when I caught Jackie's look. Air conditioners, I concluded as I shut the door, could always be replaced. Marriages were much more difficult to put back together.

I think it was Vance Havner, the sparky old pepper-'n'-salt preacher, who once commented on the need for every man to take a vacation. He tied it in with Jesus' words, "Come ye yourselves apart into a desert place and rest a while."

"If you can't 'come apart' for a rest," Havner quipped, "you'll come apart."

Our family is really good at coming apart on vacations—especially at the seams.

We finally pulled out of the carport in our six-year-old station wagon with people, suitcases, beach towels, fishing gear, food, assorted games and pediatric equipment for all those new little kittens we had to take with us. It was, I could tell, going to be a glorious time of coming apart.

Three blocks from the house our car did its own coming apart. Overworked, overloaded and overheated from sitting in the carport for two hours with the engine running and air conditioner on—because Jackie would not let the children go back in the house for fear they'd get too entrenched and want to stay—it simply gasped and stalled in the middle lane of a busy thoroughfare.

"Everybody out and push!" I shouted at my angry wife and five kids.

"Oh, Daddy," my teenage daughters moaned, "in front of everybody?"

"Push!" I screamed as horns blared and people on the sidewalk stopped and stared.

Unceremoniously, our chariot rolled to a stop on a side street while the children, mortified beyond words, crawled back into the car to await the arrival of a mechanic Jackie had gone to call.

I know nothing, absolutely nothing, about modern automobile engines. I used to be able to fix a Ford Model-A with a simple screwdriver. Now I can't even find the radiator cap. An hour later, when the cigar-chewing mechanic pulled up in a huge wrecker, I called him "sir" and asked permission to watch while he fixed what was wrong. I had some kind of horrible premonition this was just the first of a long series of events to dog us on the final leg of our "coming apart" vacation. I kept having daymares of the car stalling out again—in the toll gate on the interstate bridge or on the bow of the ferry while thirty cars behind us honked to get off.

Switching his cigar from one side of his mouth to the other, the mechanic uttered a few guttural sounds, took his pliers and pounded on the top of the carburetor. "Now try it," he said, wiping his greasy hands on his shirt. It started right up.

I gave him his $47 check and put the car in reverse. It stalled again. Jackie went running down the street hollering at the departing mechanic. "Hey, mister, sir, please—"

He returned, hit the carburetor with the pliers again and said, "Now try it," which I understand is the first phrase all mechanics learn in the Mr. Goodwrench mechanics' school, like dump-truck helpers learn to say, "C'mon back, c'mon back."

We "tried it again" and it worked beautifully. He set the idle so it sounded as if it was going forty miles an hour even while we were stopped, said to cut off the air conditioner at every stop light, and concluded, "My advice is to keep it running until you get to where you're going."

"Where I'm going," I muttered in exasperation, "is back to the house to unpack. I didn't want to go to that dumb autograph party in the first place—"

"Please, Honey," my wife begged, "don't take it out on the children. You've been promising them this coming apart for months."

"I've already come apart," I said.

But I gave in. I always do. We backed our rusting, creaking car out into the roar of traffic and headed north again. We were three hours late, everyone was hot, hungry and angry, and one of the kittens had disappeared. I convinced the children it was probably under the spare tire (it was) and we'd find it when we stopped for the night.

"We'll have to take turns going out every two hours during the night to put gas in the car in order to keep it running all night," I said sarcastically.

"Or," my wife said sweetly, "we can just drive all night long like we used to do when the kids were little. But you're probably too old to do that now, aren't you?"

We drove all night long.

When God told Adam that he was going to have to work the rest of his life, I think He was actually doing him a favor. I know. These resting spells are about to wear me out.

Mountain Religion

The fellows came to mow my North Carolina pasture yesterday afternoon. I've been alone in the mountains for about a week, living in our little vacation cottage and working on a book manuscript.

The hay was up to the haunches on the ponies and needed to be cut. Ordinarily I wouldn't pay much attention to the haycutters, but my shoulders were aching from sitting long hours in front of my word processor. The sun was just setting in the western sky, sending rays of burnished gold streaming over the mountains, and I needed to get up and stretch my legs. Besides, I hadn't talked to anyone in two days. Since one of the men was leaning on a fence post while the other worked the tractor, it looked like a good chance to hear a human voice.

The fence-post leaner was a welder by trade who mowed pastures after work. Born and raised "just across the holler," he was full of mountain wisdom. When he found out I was a "preacher," he wanted to talk religion.

"We got two kinds o' churches in this place," he said. "Dead 'uns and live 'uns. The dead 'uns don't bother nobody, but the live 'uns is always fightin' each other somethin' fierce."

I allowed how that was something that seemed to be going on all over the kingdom, so he kept talking. It seems they had just finished a big fight over at Hebron Church. Hebron, you remember, was one of the old cities of refuge set up under the administration of Joshua. It was to be a place of peace. But this mountain Hebron was anything but that, according to the haymower.

"It seems that half the folks wanted to throw the pastor out," he said, "while the other half wanted to keep 'im. So they went stormin' outten the church house and had a big free-fer-all on the front lawn. Some of 'em got ter hittin' each other with thar fists. And women, tew. You never seed the like o' them women, hittin' at them men and pullin' at each other. My nephew's been after me to come to church with 'im, so me and the wife were visitin' that Sunday. My nephew was one o' them fer the pastor and he was right in thar with the rest, swingin' his fists and stompin' with his boots. We're glad we got outten thar alive."

My friend reached over and pulled a hay stalk out of the ground, peeled it back and stuck it between his teeth.

"Well, somebody finally called the sheriff and he came up with his siren a-blowin' and stopped the fight. Then he got up on the hood o' his car and told them folks how sorry they was and that they should all go home and pray. I don't rightly recollect what the inside sermon was about that mornin', but that outside sermon the sheriff preached was about the best I'd ever heard."

About that time something broke on the tractor and my friend had to go out in the pasture to see about it. I returned to my studio, glad that I had a chat with him. He seemed to have his head screwed on straight, although he was thoroughly confused over the way some of God's folks act sometimes.

Who ain't?

Anyway, other than that—and the big explosion day before yesterday when the revenooers blew up a still down in the valley and the gunshots over in the cemetery durin' a funeral—things have been peaceful around here. After all the fightin' on TV over the television evangelists, I had considered visiting one of the area churches this Sunday. Now, after talking to the haymower, I think I'll just stay home, read my Bible and see what God has to say to me. I just don't know how much mountain religion a man can take.

Dawg Days

Here in the mountains of Western North Carolina, "Dog Days" officially began on July 28. The local folks, many of whom I've known since I started spending my summers here as a seven-year-old boy in 1939, tell me they last forty days. They begin when the Dog Star makes its bright appearance over the eastern horizon.

The Romans, someone said, gave the star the name of Sirius, or Dog

Star. They blamed it for the arrival of the hot, muggy weather. But here in the mountains Dog Days have other meanings. Here the mountain people speak a pure language flavored with ancient Cornish and Celtic idioms and just enough fables and folklore to keep flatland touristers like me coming back for more.

"You'uns got Dawg Days down thar in Florida? We'uns shore hate to see 'em get har."

Our down-the-road neighbor, who was born right here in this cove, started the whole thing last week by reminding me that whatever weather you have the first day of Dog Days will be a good sign of the weather for the next forty days.

I went to bed last night thinking about Aunt Lou Summey, who lived on top of the mountain near the big walnut grove, up the dirt road from our cabin. One summer back in the '40s, when my little brother and I were running barefooted through the mountains dressed in overalls and sucking on hay straws, Aunt Lou scared the britches off us with some of her high-flying stories.

"Lots o' dawgs go mad durin' Dawg Days," she wheezed one evening, sitting on her rickety old porch near the grape arbor. My little brother, John, and I were sitting on the big stone that acted as a step to her porch. Down in the holler the evening fog was creeping up the mountain, and we were huddled together, listening.

"Not only dawgs, but coons, bats and even foxes. Why, I seen a big old red fox come stalkin' up the road one e'en, just about this time o' day. Hit was just twilight and I could see his lips a-snarlin' and his fangs a-drippin' white foam. He'd already bit three young'uns down thar in the holler and was a-comin' after me. He was jest fixin' to leap at my throat when my son, Jesse, blasted the critter with the scattergun. You'uns shore better watch out fer wild critters when you go home t'nite. They'll leap fer your throat outta the fog and get you'uns fer shore."

We'uns set all kinds of sprint marks running home that night from Aunt Lou's house.

It was Herschel Lee's wife, Lee-Lee, who told us kids that nothing would heal during Dog Days. "Now that's the gospel truth," she told John and me as we sat wide-eyed in her dirt yard while she boiled sheets in a big, black iron kettle over an outside fire. "You'uns run a briar twixt your toes and hit'll not heal fer forty days. Hit's the dew. You

113

get dew in yer scratches and they'll jest fester. A-sides that, if'en you stub your toe during Dawg Days, the nail'll always fall off. Hit's the gospel.''

My brother John is now a medical doctor. We never talk about it, but I'll bet he still believes—despite what he learned in medical school—that your toenail will always fall off if you stub it during Dog Days.

Like most kids, I was indoctrinated with a lot of what people called ''gospel'' in my childhood—not just about mad foxes and briars between my toes, but about God's judgment, the second coming, and what you have to do to be saved.

No amount of seminary or Bible study has been able to separate me from all my superstitions. After all, if it was good enough for ''them,'' it's good enough for me—even if it was all mixed up and ain't true. Yet, it's still kinda' fun to believe—if you know what I mean.

So, despite the superstition and folklore, I still love Dog Days. It's like going to a Pentecostal camp meeting and listening to the preachers, or going down to my mother-in-law's Primitive Baptist Church for their annual ''All Day Preachin' and Dinner on the Grounds.''

But up here—when it's ''lay-by'' time on the farm and folks have enough time to sit a spell on the front porch, rock and talk, chaw and spit, spin a few yarns and watch the stars come up in the evening— Dawg Days bring back a raft of memories.

It's time for the sweet corn to ripen, for big, green, ripe watermelons and plump, frying-size chickens. It's time for honey in the comb, tying strings on June bugs, chasing lightning bugs and watching the old mules turn the sorghum mill so you can sip 'lasses like you never tasted. It's time to rope off the main street downtown on Monday night and join the cloggers as they make music on the pavement. It's time for ''protracted meetings'' in the brush arbor, all-day singings and dinner on the grounds, picnics in the holler, long tables set up on saw horses sagging under the weight of more food than you can even dream about, hayrides on country roads, apple cider, and so many churns of homemade ice cream that you have to unbutton your pants and let your belt hang loose.

I hate to leave them behind—these Dog Days. But that's because it's so much easier to believe a fable than the truth. I cut my teeth on mountain fundamentalism—a fundamentalism mixed with fear and superstition.

But it also contained a pure gospel—pure like the language of the folks in the hollers. The problem with folk gospel is the same one the farmers face at the sorghum mill: how to separate the juice from the pulp, how to burn off the impurities so you won't scorch the molasses, and finally how to get the real stuff to the market at a price people can afford.

It's worth it, however, for despite the fun of half-believing all the Dog Days theology, only the truth makes you free. It was Josh Billings, I believe, who said, "I'd rather know a few things for certain than be sure of a lot of things that just ain't so."

Next week I return to Florida, where I'll face an even more confusing mixture called God and mammon.

That is, I'll make it home lessen' that critter I sees comin' up the path through the fog is a big ol' red fox with white foam a-drippin' from his fangs. If it is, I ain't a-waitin' around to see what's truth and what ain't.

And that's the gospel.

Skip Day

"Next Thursday is Skip Day," my fifteen-year-old daughter, Sandy, announced before leaving the house for another exciting day at Johnson Junior High.

"Is that an approved holiday?"

"Of course not," she giggled. "If it were approved it wouldn't be any fun. But they've always had one—just like they did when you were in school. Last year the kids all went out to Judge Woodson's and swam in his pool. This year I've invited them to our house."

"All 1,500 of them?" I screamed.

"It's only the ninth-grade class," she laughed. "Besides, I'm class president. It goes with being a leader, Dad."

Fortunately, only forty of the 500 showed up. The rest headed for the beach. And they had to change it to Friday. The word was out the principal had learned it was planned for Thursday and was going to catch them.

That made it even more fun.

What I didn't know was the principal took it seriously. Five hundred kids out of school meant the loss of mucho state and federal dollars.

Skip Day was definitely not an approved holiday.

Forty kids in a swimming pool are a lot of kids. My wife gave orders before leaving for her midday appointment at the hairdresser. One kid on the slide at a time. Don't run around the pool. After lunch put all garbage in the cans. And most important, do not use the pool as a bathroom. Then she headed for the beauty parlor, leaving me in charge and my college-age daughter, Bonnie, acting as the lifeguard. I went inside to my studio. Skip Day could get along very well without me.

Right at noon I heard a mighty shriek go up from the backyard. Fearing the worst, I dashed out of the house in time to see the kids fleeing in all directions—into the woods, across the pasture, behind the garage.

I grabbed one of the young girls as she screamed past. "What's going on?"

"The principal's here!" she shouted, pulling loose and heading for the tall pine trees behind the barn.

I dashed around to the front of the house. I had never met the principal before, but there was no mistaking who he was. Principals, well, principals just look like principals. He was just getting out of his car along with the dean—whom I had heard of but never met either. They were marching across my lawn heading for the front door. I knew it was the dean because he looked just as Sandy had earlier described him—a cross between a gorilla and a bulldozer.

Suddenly I was running, too. Back into the house and up the stairs. It wasn't until I was in the closet that I realized this was my own house—and I was the owner. Sheepishly I went back down and answered the front door.

"A reliable and loyal student told us that Sandy had invited the entire freshman class to your house to break the law," he said sternly. "School board regulations strictly forbid this kind of thing. If you like, I'll send you a copy."

"No need," I sighed, wondering if he ever skipped school when he was a boy.

"You need to know, sir, that we take this extremely seriously," the serious principal said seriously. "We do not condone breaking laws as some people seem to do."

"I'll send them back to school," I said with resignation.

"I knew you would cooperate," he said, motioning to the huge dean who lumbered behind him back out to his car.

It took a half hour to get everyone back together. By then half of them had gone in other directions—most having left to go to the beach. I preached them a little half-hearted sermon, telling them that, as the principal had to submit to the authority of the school board, so I had to submit to the authority of the principal. They had to leave.

Churches are not the only places you find people who can't bend without breaking. You find them in schools, too.

No one seemed to be disappointed. Being caught just made it that much more memorable. The handful that was left piled in a pickup truck and a couple of station wagons, one of them driven by my daughter Bonnie, and headed back to school—by way of the beach. They felt honor bound, Sandy said, to round up the rest of the kids and encourage them to return to school, even if it took the rest of the afternoon.

I returned to my studio. Still shaking. I spent the next hour dreaming of all the smart things I wish I had said to the principal—but was too shaken to think of at the time. You never outgrow being afraid of the principal.

SEVEN

The Great Outdoors

Only a Fool Would Try
To Paddle Down That River

The Econolockahatchee River (affectionately called the Little Econ by the Florida white man who never could pronounce those Seminole words) is one of ten rivers officially designated as Wilderness Canoe Trails by the Florida Division of Parks and Recreation. It begins south of State Road 50 east of Orlando and terminates at the St. John's River, twenty-eight miles downstream. According to the little brochure published by the recreation department, the estimated time to cover the distance in a canoe is nine hours.

That is, if you paddle like crazy, if there are not forty trees which have fallen across the river, if a water moccasin doesn't fall in the canoe, and if you don't have to leave the canoe after dark and walk out through the cypress swamp.

Early one Friday morning my two boys—Bruce, sixteen, and Tim, eleven—helped me unload the canoe from the top of the car and slip it gingerly into the dark brown water at the starting point under a highway bridge about thirty miles from our house.

Jackie stood beside the car, staring into the dark woods where the winding river disappeared into the trees. "Only a fool would try to paddle down that river," she muttered.

"I'm doing it for the boys," I said. "They'll remember this experience the rest of their lives. We'll stop and cook lunch on the river bank, enjoy nature and meet you at 5 p.m. downstream."

"What happens if you're not at the finish place by dark?" Jackie asked as she turned the car around to head back home. Our plan was for her to spend the day shopping, then meet us at the bridge just below where the Little Econ empties into the huge St. John's.

"We've given ourselves an extra hour," I said, "so we'll probably be there before you are."

With Bruce at the bow paddle and Tim in the middle, we shoved off. Immediately we were swallowed up in one of the most beautiful cypress swamps I'd ever seen. But something was wrong. The little brochure we'd received from the Division of Parks and Recreation failed to mention that a lot of trees had fallen down across the river. By a lot I mean about forty. That meant at every windfall we had to pull the canoe up against the bank, get out and carry it around the fallen tree. Sometimes the next fallen tree was just yards downstream, meaning we had to do it again or just keep on pulling the canoe through the thick underbrush.

Canoes, we quickly discovered, do amazingly well in the water. But trying to pull one behind you over cypress stumps and through palmetto patches is a different matter, especially if your eleven-year-old son is tired and insists on sitting in the canoe as you drag it along the ground.

By mid-afternoon we had gone four miles and were muddy, scratched and exhausted from all the pulling, tugging, carrying and occasional paddling. "We'll never make it," Bruce moaned from his bow position, pushing off on a big stump that had fallen into the narrow river.

He was right. When night falls in the Florida swamps, it falls like Ker-Boom! The river had grown swifter and deeper, the windfalls were more plentiful, and we had decided it was easier to squeeze under most of the logs than it was to get out and drag the canoe around. That is, until we tried to squeeze under the log where the water moccasin was resting on top.

I didn't know he was there until the bow of the canoe was already under the log. Bruce, who had hunkered down in the front and slid under the log with the bow of the canoe, was now out of sight from where I was sitting in the stern. With the canoe now wedged under the log, Tim stood up in the middle to help push it along. That was when I heard Bruce's terrified scream from the other side of the log.

"Snake!"

No word strikes more terror into the heart of a canoeist than the word "Snake!"

"Where?" I screamed back.

"In here!" Bruce shouted from the other side of the log. Then I heard him jump overboard.

"Jump! Jump!" he screamed as he flailed away in the chest-deep water. "He's in the boat."

I made a decision a long time ago that if a snake ever wanted my boat he could have it without an argument.

"Jump!" I shouted at Tim.

He didn't need any encouragement and did a backdive into the river. I followed him, but when I did the canoe rebounded against the underside of the log, bounced high in the air and turned over in the water. Now the snake was no longer in the canoe, but in the water with us.

I've never seen as much activity in such a short period of time. Screaming and beating the water with our hands, we headed for the bank. Bruce made it first. Grabbing a big stick he looked wildly in all directions. The snake had disappeared.

So had the canoe. It had popped out on the other side of the log and was floating downstream, filled with water. I raced along the bank after it, my shoes filled with water, and finally caught up with it as it turned sideways in a bend of the river. Jumping into the water, I pulled it to shore.

Fortunately, what little gear we had was still under the seats of the canoe. Bruce and Tim, still wide-eyed and pale-faced, joined me and helped me turn it over and empty the water.

Just then Bruce spotted the snake again, floating down the river behind the canoe. Screaming, he grabbed his big stick to protect himself in case it came ashore.

But it had no intention of coming ashore. Big, old, rotten vines don't swim. The more we looked at it the more we realized it wasn't a snake at all. It was a piece of a big vine that had fallen out of a tree and landed on the log over the stream. When Bruce had pushed off from the log he had dislodged the vine, which upon falling into the canoe, had grown fangs and become a four-foot cottonmouth water moccasin.

"Well, it looked like a snake," Bruce said.

We all agreed that we would have done the same thing if that vine had dropped in our laps off a log.

But by then the sun was low in the sky. We estimated we had traveled six miles in ten hours. The safest thing to do was to beach the canoe and walk out. Besides, none of us wanted to run the risk of a real snake winding up in the canoe with us—especially at night.

Our little map showed us that four miles downstream was a county road bridge. But unless you have ever tried to walk four miles in a cypress swamp in the dark, it can take all night. The half moon gave us just enough light to see the sinkholes and to convince us that every stump was a black bear, but not enough to keep us from tripping over logs or running into huge spider webs. There are very few sensations to match running into a spider web at night, knowing one of those fuzzy things the size of your hand is now crawling around on your shirt in the dark. I had heard of people going mad when lost in the swamps, and I was gradually beginning to believe it could happen.

We followed the twisting river the best we could in the dark, stepping in deep mudholes and sometimes battling our way through saw palmettos over our heads. The mud helped cake the blood from the scratches, so we weren't too bad off. But after getting lost and crossing the same log three times Tim said, "Daddy, I think we ought to stop and pray."

Well, I had been doing a lot of praying already, but I agreed. Bruce put the final touch on the prayer by saying, "And by the way, thank You, Lord, that there really aren't any dragons."

We all laughed and at just that moment a stray range cow, which had been standing silently just a few feet from us, decided it was time to moo. Loudly. We all screamed and I wildly swung a canoe paddle in the direction of the moo, hitting Bruce on the shoulder. He thought the dragon had grabbed him and he knocked Tim down as he tried to get away. The cow, totally terrified, went crashing off through the brush, giving the impression more dragons were on the way. It took a long time to find our hearts, which had leaped out of our chests and climbed the nearest tree.

At 10:30 p.m. we finally burst out of the woods on Highway 419—eighteen miles south of our intended destination. A scraggly trio, we examined ourselves for dragon bites and then stood alongside the bridge with our thumbs out until a pickup truck gave us a ride down the road to a service station that was closed for the night.

"There's a pay phone outside," the driver said. "Your wife'll probably be glad to know you're still alive."

I made a collect call home. Jackie was in bed asleep.

"I talked to a man where you were supposed to come out," she mumbled. "He said he made that trip last year and it took him two-and-a-half days to get out of the swamp. I decided to come on home and go to bed."

"Well, send somebody after us," I said. "We'll be sitting here on the curb at the gas station."

While we were waiting, courage returned and Bruce volunteered to come back the next day—in the daylight and with a friend—to bring the canoe out.

"Don't you think someone might steal it before then?" Tim asked.

"Not a chance," I said. "Only a fool would try to paddle down that river."

One More Night in the Swamp

DATELINE: Florida Swamps. Here we are, deep in the jungle on a romantic family camping trip. We arrived last evening and already I'm a great mass of welts and scratches.

"It's too early for mosquitos," I had told my wife. "Besides, we don't have room for that mosquito spray anyway."

Ten thousand times those words came back to haunt me last night as eight of us tried to crowd into our borrowed nine-by-nine tent. We tried everything, even the power of positive singing, to make the night go faster. "Sing and smile and pray," we sang loudly at 1 a.m., "the bugs will go away." But they didn't.

We unrolled our borrowed sleeping bags and found they were filled with mildew. It didn't make any difference, because in a nine-by-nine tent the only way eight people can sleep is standing up.

"Let's find some primeval plot in the wilderness," I had suggested when the subject of a spring vacation came up, "and get alone with God and nature while the children are out of school."

It was a terrific idea, only so far we've had multitudinous experiences with nature and very little communion with God. Maybe that will come today after the sun has dried out the matches (oh yes, it rained last night, too) and Jackie drives back into town to get some insect repellant and poison-ivy medicine. Strange, how these things hamper your ability to worship.

We did have a few romantic moments last night as we cooked around the campfire. We had borrowed a gas camp stove, but I tried to light it and burned my eyebrows off in a terrific explosion. So we cooked over the campfire.

"The rugged woodsmen," I told my excited children, "cook pork and beans by putting the can right down in the fire."

Things went very well until I tried to get the can out of the fire and blistered my fingers. Bruce then got the pliers out of the car (we started carrying pliers after we discovered we needed them to bang on the carburetor to get the engine started) and helped me grab the can and pick it up out of the coals. That was when we discovered the fire had melted the solder around the bottom, and when Bruce picked up the can with the pliers, the beans stayed in the fire.

We finally roasted hot dogs on palmetto sticks. Not bad, considering the buns were a little soggy from having fallen in the lake.

"I can remember as a boy," I had told my wife, "camping in the mountains of North Carolina. There's nothing better than waking to the aroma of frying bacon."

"Try me," Jackie said. "I'd be glad to waken to the aroma of frying bacon if I could just get to sleep in the first place."

It was, indeed, a wild night. It wasn't just the mosquitos, either. Just about the time things calmed down and the mosquitos went off to sharpen their beaks, Bonnie screamed in the darkness, "Something hairy just ran across my neck."

That started all the other children screaming. My wife, who was scrunched into the one-man sleeping bag with me, suddenly leaped to her feet and started flailing the inside of the tent with both hands. "It's on me, too!" she screamed.

That wakened the mosquitos who returned in force.

It was an hour before things got back to normal, at which time Tim announced he had to go to the bathroom. Well, there aren't such things as bathrooms in the jungle, meaning he had to unzip the tent and go out in the darkness to tinkle. It also meant I had to get up and go outside with him, for no normal eight-year-old boy is going to do that kind of thing without his daddy—especially in the middle of the night in the jungle.

"Make sure you zip up the tent when you go out," Jackie said from her wide-awake position beside me. "If you let another one of those hairy things in like you did last time I'm going home right now. And you better believe me."

I believed her and zipped the tent behind us as we headed for the bathroom. I was standing up sleeping, waiting for Tim to finish, when I heard him scream, "Bear!"

The only thing that strikes more terror in the heart of a camper than a child screaming, "Bear!" is to be in a canoe stuck under a log and hear a child scream, "Snake!"

Of course, everything looks like a bear at night—especially a big stump next to the tent. Only in this case, Tim had not finished going to the bathroom, and when he saw the bear he did what any eight-year-old kid would do: He turned toward his father—which meant my leg was now anointed from the knee down with nature's mosquito repellant.

Of course, the cries of "Bear!" woke everyone in the tent who started screaming things like "Where?" and "Help!"

The problem was—that big, old, black stump did look like a bear. I couldn't understand why it didn't move. Obviously it was waiting for us to flee, then it would attack us with its claws and fangs. Holding Tim, who was holding on to my wet leg, we edged slowly to the door of the tent, gingerly working with the zipper.

Just then Bruce came bursting out of the tent, flashlight in hand, shouting, "Where's the bear?"

I almost—almost—wet my other leg.

"Over there," Tim said, now brave since a flashlight was burning. Bruce pointed the light at the stump and let out a hysterical laugh.

"He was sitting on the stump," Tim said. "You scared him away."

Fortunately, everything looks better in the daylight.

Early this morning I sneaked off, like Thoreau, to do some creative writing in the woods. Despite the fact I smelled like a smokehouse and had somehow or another managed to get a melted marshmallow in my hair during the night, I looked forward to those few moments of quiet communion. However, the log I chose to sit on was filled with fire ants, and I came screaming back into camp, tearing at my clothes and heading for the lake. I doubt seriously if I get much done during these days of family togetherness and harmony with nature.

If the thrashing about I hear in the underbrush isn't a bear or a panther, I'll try to jot down some spiritual profundities and share them with you at a later time. Right now I'm not in much of a mood to do anything except go home.

Dads: God's Gift to Nature

My knowledge of nature is formidable, even if I do say so myself. Few men can spot a tiger quicker than I can. Unfortunately, there are no tigers to be found in our camping area in the swamp. I am also an expert on elephants, zebras, hippos and gorillas. All evening I have been looking for something like this in order to regain my children's respect for me as a nature expert. Their "Daddy, what's that?" questions prod me to spout forth sage answers based on my vast jungle experience. But it's embarrassing for me to point out an object in the lake as an alligator, only to have my nine-year-old daughter wade out and pick up a submerged palm frond.

I'm fairly good on birds. I'm pretty hard to fool when it comes to identifying a solid red bird; or one that has a red breast; or one that has great big talons, a great beak, a tremendous wingspread and appears on our money. But it seems that we've pitched our tent in the midst of a migration of the oddest species of birds I've ever seen. Most of them are tiny, dull-feathered things that are forever hopping from limb to limb. I refuse to let my children think I am stupid and have finally taken to making up names such as "hammerhead hummer," "flea picker" and "bongo burpo." Happily, my image has been restored as the great white father with the red forehead and the baggy Bermuda shorts that cover mosquito-bitten legs.

I do have a few tips I would like to pass along to campers now that the season is approaching. One of them is never yield to the temptation to stretch out on your back, arms under your head, and gaze upward at the blue sky. It seems that the woods are full of little creepy things that immediately cover your body. Some of them stay with you for several days after you get home—and always seem to leave itchy spots in the most hard-to-scratch places.

I also recommend brief camping trips. This keeps you occupied. The typical three-day camping trip is composed of one day to set up camp, one day to break up camp and one day to scratch. That's about all most of us air-conditioned TV watchers can take at a time.

I also recommend taking someone along like Nancy. Nancy is the twenty-year-old ex-hippie from California who lives with us. Before her conversion to Christ, she lived in Haight-Ashbury in a hippie commune and learned all the rules of survival. Therefore Nancy was able to teach the children things like how to brush their teeth from a paper cup and occupy their hands (when all they wanted to do was scratch) by stringing beads.

Our last night in camp we did see an alligator, by the way. He was three feet long and came up to our campfire which was beside the lake. The children fed him marshmallows.

If nothing else, we have discovered that even the fiercest of creatures responds to kindness and compassion. If my children can remember that lesson, then these three days of sleepless scratching and slapping will all have been worthwhile.

EIGHT

Walkin' 'Round the Kingdom

The Happiest Day

According to my friend Ollie Swenson, who lives just down our country road, the second happiest day in his life was the day someone gave him a goat.

The happiest day was the day the goat ran away.

Ollie went on to explain how his goat—the very first day he had it—climbed the fence and ate every one of his wife's expensive shrubs, including nine hanging baskets on the patio (rope and all). The goat finished that off by devouring all the imported tulips from Holland and, without even a burp, ate one of his wife's eelskin shoes.

The next day the goat butted Ollie's mother-in-law head first into the compost pile and then totally destroyed his neighbor's garden. Two days later the neighbor called to apologize. It seems the goat—quite by accident—had gotten mixed up with two cows the neighbor was taking to the market. The goat wound up at the slaughterhouse and no one could figure out how a thing like that could have happened. Ollie said it was a time for rejoicing throughout the kingdom.

I rejoiced with him, for next to my other neighbor's peacocks—which are the noisiest, messiest, meanest birds alive—goats have no earthly good but to be contrasted to sheep.

Actually, I don't know that much about goats, but I can tell you about pigs and cows. And about horses that eat sand and have to be flushed out. Now that's quite an experience.

Mickey Evans, who runs an alcoholic rehab center on a large ranch down near Lake Okeechobee, gave me a thirty-four-year-old horse one time. The horse, he said, had been through the rehab program three times and now seemed to have its priorities straight.

One morning I walked out to the pasture behind our house to lean on the fence post, watch the sunrise and pray in the Spirit. I glanced out into the pasture and saw the horse lying on his side, looking like the Goodyear blimp. I mean he was so filled with gas he was about to float. I called the big-animal vet. He arrived within the hour.

"He's sanded," the vet said. By that he meant the horse—who no longer ate mash and got drunk—was too stupid to know the difference between grass and dirt. It seems he had eaten at least a bucket of sand. The effect was the same as pouring dirt down your sink—it had clogged his innards.

We finally got the horse on his feet, which was no easy matter. The vet told me to hold the horse's head. He then withdrew a twenty-five-foot rubber hose from his satchel and stuck it in the horse's nose. It was hard to believe. I watched, dumbfounded, as he pushed all twenty-five feet past the horse's stomach into his intestines. When all but twelve inches had disappeared, he took a large kitchen funnel and stuck it in the exposed end of the hose. He then produced a gallon jug of mineral oil. You would have had to have been there to believe it. I mean, he emptied the entire gallon into the hose. All this time the horse just stood there, looking stupid.

"That ought to fix him up," the vet said, as he began reeling in the hose from the horse's nose.

I was feeling a bit nauseated. Thinking he could get along without me, I walked around behind the horse. Just then I heard the vet scream, "Don't go back there!"

I looked up but it was too late. What happened next is too awful to describe. The effect, though, was that of standing in front of a sandblast hose. The huge explosion of gas, oil, sand and "other materials" knocked me into the barbed wire fence and left me smelling—well, it was pretty bad.

"I told you that would fix him up," the vet grinned.

It not only fixed him, but it fixed me, too. The next day, still picking strange-looking things out of my ears, I decided it was time to donate the horse to the church. But on second thought I called Mickey Evans and told him to come after the horse. The only thing that saved the horse's life was the thought of having to dig a hole big enough to bury him.

That, aside from the day I gave our two cows to Mickey, was the happiest day of my life.

Our son Tim, who always wanted to be a rancher, grew up with animals. He was constantly bringing home stray creatures—not just dogs and cats—but things like cows. One of his pets was a 2,000-pound Brahman cow named Gertie a local rancher gave him when it was a day old and its mother had died. Tim brought it home, but Jackie was the one who had to go out five times a day to feed it with a bottle. It grew to the size of our Volkswagen with horns longer than my arms. The back half of our twenty acres is fenced as pasture, but when something weighs 2,000 pounds it can eat wherever it pleases—fence or no fence. Jackie was constantly out in the yard, beating on the cow to get it out of her flowerbeds and back into the pasture.

The problem was whenever Gertie walked through the fence—as she did several times a week—the other cow, Elvira (named after my mother), followed her. Elvira enjoyed letting Gertie run interference and happily tagged along.

One afternoon Jackie was pounding on Gertie with her broom. Slowly, the cow turned and looked at her. She then lowered her head and muttered something like "I've had enough."

Reminding Gertie that she had fed and nursed her since she was a day old—a reminder the ungrateful beast totally ignored—Jackie began backing away until stopped by a fence post. Fortunately, Jackie had lost thirty pounds the year before, so when Gertie picked her up with her head, she fit right in between her horns. This made it easier for Gertie to rub Jackie up and down the fence post. Jackie was holding on to the horns with both hands, her feet off the ground, her back against the post which was wrapped with barbed wire, screaming at the top of her lungs. Two sons-in-law, Jon and Marion, heard her hollering and rushed to her rescue, pounding on Gertie until she dropped Jackie in the sandspurs and ambled back to the pasture.

The following week, not only Gertie but Elvira and the two calves were on their way to Mickey Evans' ranch. Jackie said that was the happiest day of her life.

Well, maybe the second happiest day. The happiest day was the day I gave my boat away.

You see, the problem is in owning something you have no business owning. First it was the new prop I had to buy when my son hit some rocks in the river. Then it was a new crankshaft. Last summer the boat and trailer came loose from a friend's truck and wound up in the show window of a furniture store. Since all my friends are poor and none of them has insurance (at least none of those who borrow things from me seems to have insurance), that meant I had to buy a new hull plus an eight-by-twenty-four plateglass window, a bunch of bent lawn chairs and a refrigerator with a boat-shaped dent in the door. Last month the cylinders needed re-boring, the battery died and all the steering cables rusted out.

Definition of a boat: "A hole in the water into which a fool pours his money."

No landlubber needs a boat, especially the kind that has a large engine which always quits running two miles offshore. So I had decided to give the boat to God—broken engine, rotten canvas and all.

There was a lot of thunder and lightning that afternoon. Jackie says it was because God knew the boat had a hole in it. Several holes, in fact. I'd tried three times before to give it to God. Each time He refused. I finally left it in the church parking lot with a note saying I'd stop by later for my tax receipt.

Jackie said that wouldn't work since God saw me put it there. She said all the thunder and lightning came when He saw the battery was dead, the trailer was rusted and the prop was bent.

When He realized it was going to cost more to fix it up than it was worth, He came looking for me with His two angels: Donner and Blitzen. Fortunately, I was preaching in Atlanta and He couldn't locate me.

Jackie warned me that God was going to get me back. "Not so," I argued, quoting from 2 Corinthians 9:7, " 'God loves a cheerful giver.' And no one has ever been more cheerful about a gift than I am about this one."

"Just the same," she said, "the first time He has to paddle that thing home after the engine won't start, He'll come after you."

I laughed it off and gratefully accepted my tax receipt from the church. It seems the boat was worth a lot more than I realized.

Jackie said the whole thing smacked of the time I tried to trade in my old car for a newer model. I asked the dealer if he would give me a better price if I included a used set of tires in the bargain.

"Why should I want your junk?" he asked.

It's disturbing that I often wait until a thing is almost beyond repair—or out of control—before I give it to God.

Recently a missionary family moved into our area. The church people provided most of the furnishings for their house. Everything but the refrigerator. That night at the dinner table I had a generous idea.

"Why don't we give them that brand-new refrigerator we have sitting out in our pole barn?"

"You mean the one with the boat-shaped dent in the door so it won't close?" my discerning wife smiled.

"Yeah, Dad," our teenager Bonnie chimed in, "how come you're always giving God our leftovers? I thought He was supposed to get the firstfruits."

Sometimes I don't like myself very much. I'm always trying to make a deal with God. Jackie says I'm like the little kid who took two dimes to church—one for the offering and the other for an ice-cream cone. When he accidentally dropped one coin that fell through the gutter grate in the street, he said, "Sorry, God, there goes your dime."

The dented refrigerator is still out in the pole barn. After my outburst at the dinner table I didn't have any choice but to go out and buy God's servants a new one—with an automatic icemaker.

Last year I spoke at a prayer retreat in North Carolina. The day I arrived I felt especially spiritual and promised the Lord I would give all the honorarium (I expected it to be small) to my friend Aley Gonzalez, a Filipino pastor who's doing ten times as much as I am with a thousand times less than I have. I felt really good about what I had promised God I would do.

Then they handed me my honorarium. It was for $3,000 for speaking one time.

That raised a big problem. I had something like $300 in mind. Had I only known. Then I remembered what God told Moses: "That which has gone out of your mouth I will require of you." It seemed better to keep my promise than to have God "require" it from me. Aley got his money and I paid for my own way home.

Bonnie was right. God doesn't want our junk.

But now I have a new problem. Yesterday Mickey called. He's bringing me a pet pig. His wife, Laura Mae, won't let him keep it in the house anymore. He said God told him to give it to me. I haven't told Jackie. She'll see it as God's way of getting even with me for the boat. In the meantime I'm trying to figure out how to get a pig in the offering plate.

Every Man's Dream

Today my friend, Brooks Watson, who lives next door, brought his backhoe out to my house and parked it in my pasture. It was like all my Christmases past wrapped into one beautiful, yellow piece of machinery.

"Sooner or later," I told Jackie, as I pulled on my backhoe shoes, "you're going to have to come to grips with a man's love of machines—and especially my obsession with backhoes."

"Why can't you be like the other men in our small group?" she asked, looking out at that beautiful, yellow earth-digger and shaking her head. "Take Gene Berrey, for instance. Gene and Jane do things together, like fishing. Al Reed helps Saundra finish antiques. Don and Linda Lees take trips together. Just because Brooks owns a backhoe doesn't mean he's obsessed with it. He doesn't even drive it. He hires someone else to do it. He and Laura go dancing together, or stay home and work on jigsaw puzzles. But not you. You want to go off by yourself on a backhoe and dig holes."

134

Jackie's right, of course. But she just doesn't understand what it's like when you spend most of your waking hours working with church committees, strong-willed staff members, and editors who are constantly revising what you have written—or sending it back for rewrites.

My obsession with backhoes goes back to the time I first started working with church people. In fact, the first year after I graduated from seminary I began dreaming I was a backhoe operator.

It was one of those recurring dreams, usually coming the night after I sat through a frustrating deacons' meeting.

In the dream I would find myself astride a huge, yellow Case or Allis-Chalmers. The legs on the backhoe would be planted soundly and I would be at the controls, touching levers, pushing pedals, digging holes and piling the dirt neatly to one side.

As soon as I got one hole dug, I would turn around in the seat, raise the legs, move the machine to another location and dig another hole.

One day I shared my dream with another Baptist preacher. He was a disciple of Carl Jung and quickly said my subconscious was digging graves for deacons.

"I don't vent my own frustrations at obstinate church members through dreams," he bragged, "but I recognize the syndrome.

"Actually," he confided, "I take out my anger on the golf course. Would you believe I have increased my drives almost seventy-five yards by imagining the golf ball is the chairman of the deacons?"

I suspected his interpretation of my dream was filtered through his own abnormalities and looked further for an explanation.

A Presbyterian pastor, an admitted Freudian, said my dream had sexual connotations. But he also believed church steeples had sexual connotations, so I knew I would have to look elsewhere for my interpretation.

Actually, it's simple. I just get tired of making decisions that are changed, revised and ignored.

For instance: It took us almost two years to install a baptistry in our church building—and I was the one who contributed the money. No one could decide whether it should be a one-stair or a two-stair model. Should it be in the middle of the platform, on the right or on the left? Should it be raised above the choir or installed level with the orchestra? Did we want it covered so the drums could sit on top of it? Where would it drain? Should it be heated? How were we going to handle that woman who insisted she paint a scene of the Jordan River on the wall behind it? Gasp!

The same is true working with editors. Nothing I write, it seems, ever goes into print the way I write it. Someone is always messing with it, taking out the cuss words, removing all the proper names of the people I like to write about—putting out the fire, so to speak. Just once I wish I could write something that would go straight from my pen into print, without having to go through the endless processes of change and revision.

No wonder I dreamed of backhoes. When you dig a hole with a backhoe, it stays dug until you turn the machine around and fill it up with the front-end loader. It doesn't argue. It doesn't talk back. It doesn't say, "Yes, but...." It just digs where you put the shovel and empties where you tell it to. And when you come out the next morning, your pile of dirt is exactly where you placed it the night before. What a wonderful sensation.

Although I stopped dreaming of backhoes years ago, my desire to own one has never left. In fact, it increases each year.

Each Christmas, I come down the stairs hoping to find a big, yellow Ford 750 with a backhoe on one end and a front-end loader on the other sitting in the driveway—with a big, red ribbon on the steering wheel. It never happens.

It's like that cowboy suit I wanted when I was six years old, the one I used to wish for on the evening star. It never materialized either.

Now here I am, grinding through middle life, wondering if I'm ever going to have my own backhoe. That's the reason today is such a good day. Brooks is getting ready to do some clearing on his property. Knowing how I've salivated for years for a backhoe, he brought his battered old machine over from his construction site and left it for me to play with for a few days before he moved it next door. What a great guy!

Several years ago, unable to afford the real thing, I bought a fifteen-horsepower Yanmar diesel tractor. It was more than a lawnmower. It came with several attachments including a bushhog and a small grading blade that fit on the back. Although I could then go out and smooth out the bumps in our long dirt driveway, the deep yearning for the genuine article—a backhoe with a front-end loader—remained.

To sit astride one of those wonderful machines, dig holes and ditches,

then pick up the dirt in the front-end scoop and spread it smoothly—
ah, that would be the ultimate.

"Tell me what you would do with it if you owned it," Jackie asked
as I headed out to the pasture, "besides spend a fortune on it every
time it broke, that is."

"I'd dig holes with it," I answered curtly—sensing the hostility which
seems to appear every time the subject comes up, which is about once
a week.

I reminded her that our children are building their houses on por-
tions of the property we've given them. "When Jon and Robin built
their house they could have saved thousands of dollars if I'd been there
to help them with my backhoe. You can use it to clear land, dig drainage
ditches, even move mountains."

"We don't have any mountains in Florida," she smiled sweetly.

"Every man needs to do something physical to serve his fellowman.
Me and my backhoe would be available to serve my neighbor, just like
the Bible commands.

"I'd take it out in our pasture and deepen our pond. I'd shape the
sides. I'd take the dirt and use it to raise the driveway so it wouldn't
be under water every time it rains. I'd go down the road and dig holes
for our friends. I'd—"

"Remember the time you got the bulldozer stuck in the bottom of
our pond," she interrupted, giggling, "and tried to pull it out with the
Datsun?"

I wished she wouldn't keep talking about the bulldozer incident. Actually, I was not the fellow who got it stuck. I had promised one of
our neighbors he could have some fill dirt. The water level was down
and the pond was dry. It was a good time to dig. So I rented a bulldozer
from the local bulldozer store.

One of the men in our church volunteered to run the machine. He
said he used to operate heavy equipment in the Army. I should have
known we were in for trouble that Saturday morning when they delivered
the big Caterpillar 'dozer and my friend took a look and said, "Where's
the steering wheel?"

Not only did he not know much about bulldozers, he was unfamiliar
with Florida soil. Down here we have sandy topsoil. Under that is a
hard clay base called "hardpan." Underneath that—sinkholes.

After an hour going back and forth across the bottom of the dry pond, pushing dirt up on the bank so it could be loaded in a dump truck, he broke through the hardpan. The bulldozer began to sink. I heard him screaming. By the time I got out in the pasture, the big machine was up to the top tread in what seemed to be quicksand. It was apparently getting ready to disappear.

That was when we tried to pull it out with the Datsun. After losing the rear bumper and stripping low gear, I called the bulldozer store.

"Happens all the time," the man said, laughing. "Just lower the blade. That will raise the treads. Put all of next winter's firewood that took you three months to split under the treads. Then the 'dozer will crawl out of the hole under its own power."

"That little Saturday afternoon episode cost you the annual royalty of two books," Jackie said. "And you want to own a backhoe?"

She just doesn't understand. What I really want is the satisfaction of doing something—anything—that doesn't get undone. And the best thing to do it with is a Massey-Ferguson. In fact, I'd settle for an old, blue John Deere.

How I envy bricklayers, painters, even dentists. When they do something, it stays done. They can go back the next day, or the next time the patient comes into the office, and nod with satisfaction.

But when you work with people, or editorial boards—.

That's the reason I need a backhoe—one of my own. Just so I can come home from a day of negotiating, walk out to the shed, climb up on that big, beautiful, yellow piece of machinery, turn the switch, hear it roar to life, lumber out to dig a ditch, move a pile of dirt, dig up a tree stump, and know it will do exactly what I tell it to—without talking back.

"That is, until it breaks," Jackie said.

I hate it when she brings up stuff like that. "Do you remember what Stan Elrod told you last year when you asked him to try to find you a used backhoe up in Charlotte? I couldn't believe you were serious. You actually thought you could fly up there and drive that thing all the way to Florida—600 miles on the interstate."

Stan is a builder in Charlotte, North Carolina. I knew where Jackie was going and told her, frankly, it was not right to talk about a friend behind his back. She ignored me.

138

"He reminded you how he almost bought one for his construction company. Then he figured out how much it would cost initially plus how much it would cost to fix it since they're always breaking down. He said you could rent one every weekend for a hundred weeks and still be better off than if you had bought one."

I know better than to argue with someone who is insensitive, nonvisionary, dogmatic and stubborn—especially when she's right.

Jackie went ahead to remind me of the fellow we hired to enlarge our pond several years ago. He showed up with an ancient dragline. The second day of work he got his bucket stuck in the mire on the bottom of our pond and the boom on his dragline bent, like a kid bends a soda straw. That disabled monster sat in our backyard for three months—the big, old bucket rusting in the muck on the bottom of our pond, its bent boom hanging pathetically like the broken wing of a bird. Every night I stood in my backyard looking at it, knowing it was going to cost thousands of dollars to fix, and gave thanks it didn't belong to me.

But that was a dragline. Those things are always breaking down. Backhoes, I'm convinced, are a different story. Besides, I don't intend to buy one—at least not a new one. I'm trusting God to give me one. And how can a man turn down a gift from God?

You see, a man really doesn't need a reason for digging holes. In fact, holes are an end in themselves—not a means to some other end. That's the reason I can hardly wait to get up on Brooks's big old machine and start to work. I'll probably go back tomorrow and put the dirt back in the hole. Then I'll start to work digging out all those tree stumps that keep knocking my lawnmower blade out of line. After that I'll start to work on the network of drainage ditches needed to drain my property. I'll probably want to reshape the pond. A kidney shape would look nice, I think, with a little humpback bridge over to the island I'll build in the middle. My neighbors will call on me, asking me to come down and help them pull down a tree, dig up a palmetto patch or level off their driveway. I'll be the most wanted and most admired man in the community. In fact, I may never write anything else the rest of my life— that is, until my editors come begging, promising never again to change what I've put on paper.

God understands—even if my wife doesn't—how desperately I need, every once in a while, to do something with my own hands that will be the same tomorrow as it was today.

That can only be accomplished if I own a backhoe.

Star light, star bright,
First star I've seen tonight.
I wish I may, I wish I might,
Have the wish I wish tonight.
BACKHOE!

No Smoking

Living with Jackie is like living with a fire extinguisher. It's probably something she inherited from her daddy, who was a fireman. But she hates smoke—especially the kind that comes from smoldering tobacco leaves.

On our very first high school date—I was sixteen and she was fifteen— she snatched a cigarette out of my mouth and crushed it on the ground with a vengeance. I knew then I was in for a lifetime of battling if I decided to keep on smoking. But I had no idea she not only intended to straighten me out, she was willing to take on the entire smoking public.

Even though I gave it up before I really got started, I still like to recall, every now and then, the macho feeling of lightin' up a Lucky, shaking a Camel out of the pack and blowing smoke out of my nose in front of my buddies, and saying, "Ahhh! Smooth!" when I inhaled an Old Gold.

"Gross!" Jackie sneers, when I talk like that. "What's manly about yellow teeth, breath that smells like the inside of our trash compactor, and having to stop in the middle of a kiss to cough and spit?"

I hate it when she talks like that. I'd rather remember it the way I wanted it to be—rather than the way it really was.

My sophomore year in college I decided, along with a million other sophomores, to take up pipe smoking. Sophomore pipe smoking is a disease that sweeps through college campuses—usually in the fall— infecting young men by the millions, much like Dutch Elm disease infects trees. Freshmen seldom smoke pipes. Nor do men who work for a living. Pipe smoking is for philosophers, professors and liberal preachers. It's also for sophomores.

My model that year was a fellow ATO named Jerry Conner. We called him the Colonel. He wasn't a real colonel. He wasn't even a Kentucky Colonel like Grandpa Thompson. But he looked like a colonel, and besides that, he was going to law school. He also smoked a pipe. Three weeks into my sophomore year, I went down to the local tobacconist and bought all the equipment necessary to make me look like the Colonel:

- a $35 brier pipe,
- a package of pipe filters,
- a package of pipe cleaners,
- a chrome tamper which had something called a scraper on the other end,
- a fancy lighter which produced a flame in the middle so I could light my pipe on a windy day while dressed in a trench coat standing on a bridge over the Thames River looking thoughtfully at the Tower of London,
- and a pouch of apple-flavored tobacco.

If I couldn't match the Colonel, I could at least look like Sherlock Holmes.

I only smoked it twice. The Colonel forgot to tell me never to tilt my head back so the bowl of the pipe was higher than the stem. Pipes, I've since discovered, should always be tilted down. The only ones to be tilted up are corncob pipes like General MacArthur used. Corncob pipes on long, thin stems are designed to be held tightly between your teeth to give you a jaunty, arrogant image. But farmers and legendary generals know they should never be lit, especially when wading through the surf of the South China Sea while saying, "I have returned!"

The thing I discovered as a college sophomore is that, once a pipe is lit, it immediately collects a small amount of horrible-tasting, bitter juice in the stem. If you tilt it back, as I did after about twenty minutes of sitting around puffing and rubbing my chin (as pipe smokers are wont to do), the horrible juice runs into your mouth. When that happens you immediately give up pipe smoking forever. Which is what I did.

It's sad, for pipe smoking is a great art and only a few men, like the Colonel, seem to have ever mastered it.

We had another fellow in the fraternity, the Rev. Francis Woolsley, who took up pipe smoking as a career, eventually rising to the position of dean of a small New England college. Francis was studying, he told us when he arrived at our small Georgia Baptist college from

Connecticut, to become a Congregational pastor. Since no one in Georgia had ever heard of the Congregational Church (every living creature in Georgia, even the heathen, is a Baptist), we assumed Congregationalists all smoked pipes. The ATOs, in particular, were impressed. The Colonel only smoked occasionally; Francis was a serious pipe smoker.

It was soon evident Francis was using his pipe smoking to offset his stupidity, which is true of a number of pipe smokers. Unable to think things out rationally, he mastered the two facial expressions that traditionally go with pipe smokers: thoughtful and bemused. Those were the total ingredients of his success. I mean the fellow was just plain dumb. One of my fraternity brothers who came from the swamps down near Ludowici, Georgia, said that, in his considered opinion, if intelligence were crankcase oil, Francis didn't have enough to wet the tip of his dipstick—let alone reach the add-one-quart mark. However, since he was able to master the art of pipe smoking, Francis made an excellent dean.

I spent two hours with him once, many years later, in his foul-smelling office on the third floor of the administration building on the little campus in western Connecticut. No matter what problem was brought before Dean Woolsley, his response was to sit back and puff on his pipe, alternating his expressions between thoughtful and bemused. I kept thinking that if he ever decided to give up his deanship he could always become a successful attorney dealing with wills and divorces. That doesn't take much intelligence either, but it does mean you have to project a certain image. It's all wrapped up in pipe smoking.

During the two hours I spent in Dean Woolsley's office he had only one visitor—a freshman from Vermont who was having trouble with his class schedule. Francis spent the entire twenty minutes the intimidated student was in his office giving the lad his bemused expression. The poor student, standing before the dean's desk and shifting his weight from one foot to the other, stammered out his problem. All the while Francis kept fiddling with his pipe. He fumbled about in the pockets of his old tweed jacket looking for his tobacco pouch. Then he spent a lot of time scraping the inside of the bowl, getting rid of a lot of collected tars and other horrible accumulations. Occasionally he would glance up at the student with his bemused-thoughtful expression, nodding as if he really understood. That was followed by a long period

142

of filling his pipe—tamping and filling, tamping and filling—interspersed with thoughtful looks up from his task. I can't tell you how impressed I was, especially since I knew Francis Woolsley was just plain dumb. Then he began probing his upper pockets for a match. Finding one at last, he struck it, using the underledge of his desk. Then he leaned back in his creaky, old, wooden swivel chair—sucking and puffing, sucking and puffing, sucking and puffing.

By that time the poor student was almost in tears. Looking up, holding his pipe in one hand, Dean Woolsley stroked his chin and nodded again, giving the most profound bemused look I'd ever seen. This successfully suggested to the student the problem was so ridiculous that the dean was giving thought to dismissing the student from school. The poor lad—completely intimidated by the bearded dean with the huge, crooked pipe who kept blowing smoke and stroking his jaw—finally laughed feebly to indicate it was all a little joke. Then he rushed off, obviously intent on finding the solution himself. Throughout the entire process Dean Woolsley had not spoken a single word. No wonder people thought he was a genius and often wondered what great ideas he was mulling over as he puffed his pipe and looked thoughtful and bemused.

Now having set forth the wonderful advantages of pipe smoking, you probably wonder why I married a woman who is half crusader and half fire extinguisher. I once asked my psychologist friend, Harvey Hester, this same question. He mumbled something about people who commit crimes and leave obvious clues hoping to be caught, then launched into a vague theory about men wanting to marry their mothers.

He may be right on both counts. Despite my occasional temptations to sneak off and light up a Chesterfield, or to walk a mile for a Camel, I am also adamant when it comes to smoking in public places like airliners and elevators...and the cabs of pickup trucks when it's raining outside and the air conditioner isn't working and you've got to ride twelve miles into town with a lout who's smoking a three-day-old-spit-filled cigar. I mean, why does a fellow like me—who used to think the greatest smell in the world was the wafting odor of vintage tobacco from a brier pipe in a walnut-paneled den, or the nostalgic smell of a freshly lit cigarette drifting through the pine trees around an evening campfire—rejoice when the federal government finally puts a ban on smoking in airplanes? I am obviously a psychological mess.

Despite my inconsistencies, however, nobody has ever been able to accuse Jackie of being anything but a smoke fighter. I mean, nobody smokes around her—at least not for long. Either she moves or they do.

Jackie's the kind of person who, if someone asks, "Do you mind if I smoke?," answers, "I certainly do!" (with the emphasis on "certainly"). Then she stares them straight in the face until they slink away.

For years, while she has gagged, coughed and complained in the presence of smokers, I have remained silent. At a football game, sitting fifty-seven rows up with the wind blowing at thirty knots, Jackie will fan her face and say in a loud voice, "I've got to move. That man down there (pointing to a photographer on the side of the field) is smoking a cigar."

Seldom does anyone get the best of her when it comes to tobacco.

Only once, to my knowledge, did she meet her match. It happened a few weeks after we moved to our first church in South Carolina.

The church's finance committee decided to have their monthly meeting at our house. Since the house was owned by the church and the church was run by the finance committee, that meant they were like our 2,000-pound cow, Gertie, who went wherever she wanted to. That night the finance committee decided to check out their house where the new associate pastor lived with his shy, little wife. The chairman, a red-headed man by the name of Brother Pinson, who ran a little dry-cleaning establishment, called the meeting to order and lit up a cigarette.

"Don't you people have any ashtrays?" he asked, his cigarette already burning.

Jackie, who had come running from the back of the house the moment she smelled tobacco, was standing in the door of the kitchen.

"Sorry," she said, hands on hips as she glared at the man who had absolute power over my salary, "we don't have ashtrays. They encourage lung cancer. You'll either have to go outside or use my expensive china vase."

Brother Pinson, who was used to taking people to the cleaners, never blinked. Coughing (he always coughed when he inhaled), he just reached for Jackie's expensive china vase—and flicked.

After that, we had lots of little signs around the house.

"Smokers don't go to hell; they just smell that way."

"If you won't blow smoke on me, I won't vomit on you."

Gratefully, she's mellowed (slightly) over the years. She no longer throws open the window and coughs loudly when visiting in someone's home and they light up—although she may do some violent fanning if the smoke drifts in her direction.

Also, we finally bought some ashtrays—although Jackie insisted each one should have a Christian message on it. She found the ones she liked at the Jesus Junk convention in Anaheim, California. One says, "Beauty for Ashes." Another is more Pentecostal and has a Scripture reference about "tongues of fire." The one she likes best has a picture of Jesus in the bottom—right where you grind out your cigarette.

I guess part of Jackie's fanaticism has rubbed off on me. But I'm just not as demonstrative.

When a man in the elevator puffs his stinky cigar at me, I try to gag unobtrusively.

When some foul-breathed charismatic fumes his "Praise the Lord!" in my face, I hold my breath and hug him back.

And I try not to giggle when someone comes to the altar to "give it all to Jesus" and her cigarettes spill out of her purse on the floor when she kneels.

What others do is their business. It's only when they invade my airspace that I get upset. Thinking back, I'm sure I inherited that trait from my mother.

I accompanied my octogenarian mother—the one Harvey Hester said I was trying to marry when I finally gave up and let Jackie catch me—on a plane trip on her eighty-fifth birthday. Mother B, who still thinks Carry Nation (the great proponent of prohibition who used to go into taverns with her hatchet and chop up the bar) should have been named secretary of commerce, warned me before boarding the plane that if anyone blew smoke on her she'd throw up. While I try to be a gentleman around smokers, she—like Jackie—feels that ladylike behavior will only get more smoke blown in your face. Knowing this and fearing the consequences, I still agreed to accompany her that memorable afternoon on an airplane flight from her home in Florida to our mountain cabin in North Carolina.

Mother had been getting ready for the trip for months, realizing it might be her last time to see her beloved mountains. Nothing was going to interrupt her plans. My travel agent had reserved our seats at the very front of the no-smoking section, right against the bulkhead. Even so, when you are sitting in a metal tube five miles above the earth and all the windows are stuck closed and the rear end of the plane is filled with tobacco-puffers whose fumes circulate through the entire aircraft, the "no-smoking section" is something of a farce.

I tried to warn my mother of this before we boarded the plane. "I can handle it," she said.

And "handle it" she did.

Moments after the flight began I saw her fumbling with her seat belt. I knew we were in trouble. Grabbing her cane, she stumbled to her feet and stood in the aisle, facing the rear of the plane. In a voice which needed no PA system, she announced to the entire plane: "That woman back there is smoking. It's making me sick. I'm going to throw up." She got action a lot faster than the FAA. From there to Atlanta our flight was strictly nonsmoking.

Ten years before I would have been mortified by my mother's behavior. That day I joined with the fifty or so other people in the front of the plane who clapped, applauding her chutzpah.

The nonsmoker's patron saint has to be Joyce Brothers, who once told the man in front of her on the plane that if he didn't put out his cigarette she was going to vomit. He didn't. She did. Then she dumped her whoopee bag in his lap, sparking a famous lawsuit.

It was in that first church I mentioned—the one where Brother Pinson was chairman of the finance committee—that a new member came rushing into my study one morning between Sunday school and church. He said the cloud that led the Israelites through the wilderness was now hovering over our church building. I rushed out in the parking lot to see. It turned out the pillar of smoke was actually caused by a group of deacons taking a puff between the services. I'm glad I went out, because on the way back in I ran into Jackie—charging down the hall intent on speaking her piece to that group of deacons. The fact they had the power to fire me didn't faze her. She didn't see any difference in a deacon smoking on the steps of a Baptist church and a priest scratching obscenities on the wall of the Chapel of the Sistine Madonna.

Mind you, I'm not saying don't smoke. I'm just saying, if you do, please don't blow it on Jackie (or my mother) unless you enjoy being ridiculed in public.

One of my seminary professors, when asked by a young ministerial student if folks who chewed tobacco could get into heaven, replied: "Sure. The problem is they won't have any place to spit."

That, it seems to me, would be hell.

I don't think God bars smokers from heaven either. In fact, if you smoke you'll get there sooner. Yellow teeth, foul breath and lung cancer are no deterrent to God's grace. But Jackie says she just hopes He puts them all in the same room—and shuts the windows.

That, too, would be hell.

Where There's Smoke, There's Ire

Sometime between the ages of seven and seventeen, most boys (and some girls) have their first try at smoking. Like drinking beer, no one ever seems to like it in the beginning. The thrill of doing the forbidden always seems stronger than the fear of coughing—and cancer.

Sven Oleson says his two kids once found a cigarette on the sidewalk. They brought it home and sneaked off behind his tool shed to find out what smoking was all about. Cutting it in half, each lit up. Puffing, coughing and gagging, they did what the big boys do.

When they finished they sat looking at each other. Both had turned green and their eyes were swimming. Finally the littlest guy asked, "Do you feel like me?"

"What do you mean?"

"I think I just caught cancer."

No one in my family ever smoked—at least not where my mother could see them. My mother was to R.J. Reynolds what David was to Goliath. She couldn't control what went on behind her back, but no one, not even the governor, ever lit up in her house.

In fact, I remember the day the governor of Florida came to dinner. I remember him first because he told us little kids—who were peeking through the door of the living room before dinner—that everyone else had to call him governor, but we could call him Uncle Millard. My dad promised him we'd all vote for him and that seemed to make him happy.

But what I remember best was what happened after dinner. Pushing

147

back his chair, Uncle Millard reached into the inside pocket of his coat and pulled out a big cigar. As he was unwrapping the cellophane, my mother—who up until that time had been the perfect hostess—rose to her feet.

Eyes blazing, she roared, "Not in this house, sir."

Thoroughly intimidated, he instantly stuffed the cigar back in his pocket. I doubted if anyone except his own mother had ever talked to him like that. My father, embarrassed, glanced down the table at mother. She had not moved. Like Horatio in front of his bridge, Mother felt she had a divine mandate to protect our house from tobacco smoke.

My father politely rose and, clearing his throat, suggested the governor join him in a walk into the citrus grove behind the house. I followed my mother to the back door where she stood, hands on hips, making certain the cigar smoke drifted away from the house—else she would have rushed to close the windows.

Mother hated cigars as much as she hated the bourbon that was made in her native Kentucky. She punished me and sent me to my room one afternoon just for bringing home an empty cigar box to keep my marbles in. She was not only immovable—she was blatantly outspoken. As a result, by the time I was twelve I had an insatiable urge to start smoking.

A young, blond-headed buddy of mine, Jim Thompson, who grew up to be an insurance agent, told me I should try rabbit tobacco. He had smoked rabbit tobacco the summer before when he visited on his grandmother's farm in Georgia. Since we little kids couldn't buy cigarettes, rabbit tobacco was indeed the place to start.

Jim seemed to know what he was talking about. All the Georgia farm kids smoked rabbit tobacco, he said. He wasn't sure, but he imagined I could find some easily in the woods behind our house. He was so sure of himself I was afraid to let him know I didn't know what rabbit tobacco was. I never dreamed it was a hollow weed. I was as determined as I was proud, however, so one Saturday morning I walked into the woods behind our house and found what was certainly rabbit tobacco. Picking up the little brown pellets I found on the ground, I crushed them into "tobacco." Then I rolled a cigarette, using a torn piece of newspaper, and set it on fire with a big, wooden kitchen match. The result was awesome. Not only did it taste foul, it burned so fast I lost my eyebrows and almost set the woods on fire.

Later when I asked Jim how he was able actually to smoke rabbit "tobacco," I thought he would never stop laughing. He couldn't believe anyone would be so stupid as to try to smoke rabbit manure.

By the time I was fifteen I had smoked everything from grapevines to coffee grounds (the latter smoked in a homemade pipe). I had burned my tongue, scorched my throat, almost set my father's orange grove on fire and burned holes in most of my clothes.

My smoking even caused me to wreck my father's new Willys car. I had a newspaper route and I was allowed, if it was raining, to borrow his car rather than ride my big delivery bike, which had a small wheel on front to accommodate the huge wire basket where I stacked the rolled newspapers. (Later I made enough money to buy a "Whizzer" bike motor.) That morning, driving my father's new Willys through the dark, deserted streets of our little town, I lit up my homemade pipe which I had filled with Maxwell House drip-ground coffee on the way out of the house. Since coffee doesn't burn easily, you have to apply lots of heat. I had bought a new Zippo lighter but it took two hands to use it, meaning I had to steer the car with my knees; a feat not too difficult unless a honeybee flies in the window and bounces off your face, as one did that morning. That caused me to dump the now-burning coffee grounds into my lap which took precedence over everything else in the world—including the war in Korea and the fact the new Willys was headed for a huge concrete road sign.

I decided it was easier simply to bury my pants than to try to explain all the burn holes to my mother. Explaining the damage to the car was a different matter and it cost me a half-year's newspaper wages to repair it. Even so, nothing could stop me from sneaking smokes.

My big day came when, as a high school student, I swaggered up to the counter in McClure's Pharmacy and bought two plastic-tipped cigars. Cigarettes were for wimps. Real men smoked cigars. That evening after football practice I walked far back into the grove, leaned against a palm tree and became a man.

By the time I had finished the second cigar, I was in horrible shape. Full of manhood, I staggered back toward the house.

As I approached the back door, I realized I was reeking. Fearing my mother's nose for nicotine, I slipped into the house and rummaged through the kitchen cabinets for something to sweeten my breath. My

149

buddy Jim Thompson had told me that cloves were a good cover-up for tobacco smell. Finding my mother's little box of French's cloves, I figured it would probably take a handful to cover the smell of two cigars. Stuffing them into my mouth, I went into the little half-bath off the kitchen, locked the door and began chewing. Jim had failed to tell me about the chemical reaction that happens when you mix clove spit with cigars. By the time I got up off my knees (and I wasn't praying—except that I would live through the ordeal of vomiting my insides into the toilet), I vowed I'd never smoke another cigar. And I haven't.

But sadly, each generation has to learn those lessons personally.

Years later I was getting out of a taxi at National Airport in Washington, D.C., when I glanced down and saw one of those expensive cigars, the kind that come in little silver cylinders, lying on the back seat. For the same insane reason Eve plucked the apple in the garden—just to look at it—I stuck the cigar in my pocket and brought it home where I hid it in my desk. There was only one thing worse than having my mother smell tobacco on my breath, and that was having my wife find a cigar in my desk drawer.

Only it wasn't my wife who found it. It was my young teenage sons. The next day I stepped out in the backyard and heard the scurrying of feet, accompanied by loud coughing and giggling. I looked around the corner of the house and there stood my two boys, each smoking half of that cigar.

"Go to it," I told them. "Puff it good." They were startled, but when they discovered I wasn't going to punish them they picked up the cigar pieces where they had dropped them in the grass and started puffing away.

"Now you can't come into the house smelling like that," I told them as they started to turn green. "But if you'll chew on these cloves perhaps your mother won't notice the smell on your breath."

Neither boy, from that day, has ever had a desire—or even a temptation—to smoke.

Confessions of a Tomato-Hater

Every man should have something, at least one sin, that he can point to proudly and say, "That I have never done!"

Mine is: I have never—before or after marriage—eaten or even tasted a tomato. Like my mother, who at the age of ninety brags that her lips have never tasted alcoholic drink, so I am able to testify that—while billions of others since the time of Eve have unashamedly bitten into those evil, mucus-filled, squishy berries—I have remained pure, separate, apart from sin.

Recent archaeological discoveries have, you know, confirmed what many scholarly theologians have believed for centuries—that it was not an apple Satan handed to Eve in the Garden of Eden. It was a tomato which has corrupted and contaminated all mankind. Only the influence of powerful tomato lobbies has kept this information from being released to the general public.

Across the years generations of Christians have continued to eat—even at church picnics sponsored by the Women's Mission Union—the fruit of the devil. All this is given as shameful evidence of how Satan has invaded even the very heart of the kingdom of God: the covered-dish supper.

There is a fine line between self-centeredness and self-confidence, between egotism and security.

The insecure man is always afraid, often angry. The secure man faces his flaws, confesses them before the accuser gets to him (and to others) and is unashamed. He knows it is far better to risk and fail than to count himself unworthy and not risk at all.

One of the risk areas of my life is my relationship with tomatoes. I do not eat them. I have never eaten one. This is not just a religious discipline; it is made easier by the fact I cannot stand the thought of biting into one of those quivering, jellied, nauseous things. I have nothing against tomatoes per se. I imagine tomatoes were in that visionary sheet Peter saw while napping on the rooftop in Joppa—the sheet that contained all the "unclean" things of life. God, at that time, told Peter not to call anything unclean that He had created. Therefore—believing that God created tomatoes just as surely as He created rattlesnakes, mosquitos and doggie-do—I am careful not to call them "unclean" (in a spiritual sense, that is). To prove I am without prejudice I quickly point out that I love catsup—at least Heinz. In fact, as my friends can testify, I eat catsup on everything from cheese to scrambled eggs.

Some of my friends look on this as a compromise, like the time I

151

mixed wine with the grape juice in the communion service in an effort to please both the Episcopalians and the Baptists who attended our church. The result was a disaster. Every good Episcopalian knows when you have diluted the wine; and a Baptist can smell alcohol from the back pew.

But there is a vast difference between catsup and tomatoes—or at least I have so theorized, which makes me feel comfortable from a theological position.

A long time ago, however, long before I reached what the Baptists call "the age of accountability," I made a quality decision that I would never eat a tomato. And today, fifty years later, the thought of biting into one of them remains as repulsive as chewing earthworms.

Fortunately, I have been supported in this by most of the people around me. My wife knew, when she married me, that I had taken this sacred vow. Never once has she sought to dissuade me, even though I know that behind my back she does like all the other sinners: slicing and slobbering over that which my spirit labels reprehensible. The fact we have them molding and rotting in the vegetable drawer of our refrigerator, or sitting above the sink where they leak their vile juices all over the window sill, is something I have learned to live with. However, I still shudder when I come into the kitchen and find where Jackie has sliced a tomato and left the goo—some of that quivering, jellied mass that surrounds the seeds—in plain view on the countertop. I get nauseated when I pick up a paring knife and realize it has tomato excrement on the blade. But as long as I can live in the world without letting the world into me, I can get by.

I almost ate a tomato several years ago. I had ordered a hamburger at Burger King—a Whopper, no less—and specifically said to the nice young lady at the counter, "Hold the tomatoes, please." I thought at the time she looked subversive, but I was sidetracked by my children and did not do what I normally do—examine what was given me.

Instead, in good faith, I took the Whopper back to my table and sat down with my wife and children. (I can take you, even today, to the exact table where it happened.) Fortunately, we did what our family always does—we prayed together before we ate. Had we not prayed there is no telling what evil could have befallen me. Immediately upon saying the "Amen!" I bit into my Whopper. Fortunately, the Spirit of God was still on me and the gift of discernment was still active. It took only a millisecond to discover I had that foul thing in my mouth.

Like the difference between death and dying, it wasn't the thought of swallowing which terrified me. It was the thought of chewing. I remembered my father's story of the time Winston Churchill (or some other famous dignitary) attended a state dinner along with Amy Vanderbilt—the queen mother of modern etiquette. Seated beside Miss Vanderbilt, the famous leader dipped his spoon into his soup and put it in his mouth. The soup was boiling hot and Churchill, never one for pretense, noisily spit it back into his bowl. Looking over at Miss Vanderbilt, who had turned pale with shock, Churchill growled, "A fool would have swallowed it."

So with that tomato in my mouth. A less courageous man, a compromiser—realizing he had been duped by a pretty, young agent of the devil at the counter—would have swallowed without chewing. I took the manly way and spit the entire mouthful into my napkin.

That, of course, brought hilarious laughter from my children and a stern, stern, stern look from my wife. I paid attention to neither, busying myself with the process of removing the evil thing from my hamburger before it soaked into the bun—all those little seeds with mucus around them. Yuck! Then I discovered I had gotten some of it on my fork and had to wipe it off—much to the continued pleasure of my children who giggled through the entire procedure.

I'm proud to say that my example before them as a man who has kept himself pure from tomatoes remains untainted. When in my public testimony I state I have never eaten a tomato, my children step forward and confirm my position. It makes them proud that their daddy is a man of unswerving principle and courageous resolve.

It doesn't bother me that I don't eat tomatoes. I am not the least bit embarrassed to take tomatoes out of my salad and put them in my wife's bowl when we go out to eat. In fact, we have across the years worked out little procedures so I don't flaunt my goodness in front of those with less discipline. Knowing my resolve, she usually waits until someone is praying, then quite unobtrusively reaches into my salad and removes the tomatoes while all heads are bowed and all eyes are closed. She also honors me by picking those little cherry tomatoes out with her fingers—instead of spearing them with her fork, thus allowing the foul juice to leak into my salad dish.

Since the only thing worse than a raw tomato is a cooked one—especially if it is boiled with okra—I also remove them from my vegetable soup. I never make a big deal of this. Just as a nondrinker has learned to turn his wine glass quietly upside down beside his plate, so I quietly pick the cooked tomatoes out of my soup and put them in my wine glass. That way I also signal the waiter that I prefer not to drink.

I was not taught that way at home or in the seminary, nor has it been forced on me by some "shepherd." It is simply one of the things the Holy Spirit has taught me about godly living and comes as natural as saying, "No, thank you," to a whiskey sour.

But while some of my Christian friends may applaud my abstinence from hard liquor, very few understand my decision to skip tomatoes.

"What? You don't like tomatoes? What's wrong with you, anyway?"

"You eat catsup, don't you? What's the difference?"

I've heard these and every other possible remark over the more than a half-century that I have not eaten tomatoes.

I do not grow angry when questioned. I am secure.

The other day Jackie and I visited my ninety-year-old mother, who lives in the small Florida town of Vero Beach, just a few miles south of our home in Melbourne. A retired lady missionary, about the same age as my mother, was visiting with her. We took them both down to Morrison's Cafeteria for lunch.

We went through the serving line and I ordered a piece of ground steak. The woman behind the counter asked if I wanted mushroom sauce. I said yes.

I didn't know the mushrooms were cooked in tomatoes, and before I knew it she had smeared that horrible stuff all over my meat—big hunks of quivering, pink tomato in lots of juice.

I took it calmly and when we got to our table I began, as unobtrusively as possible, to take the tomatoes off my meat and put them on the bread plate.

Well, the ladies at the table thought that was awful. All of them had loud things to say about my not liking tomatoes.

My mother said it was a shame I was still like that. My wife—who is always supportive except when she gets around my mother or anyone else who thinks it's silly that a grown man doesn't eat tomatoes, at which time she becomes absolutely vicious—said I embarrassed her every time we went to a restaurant. The elderly missionary lady said if I lived overseas long enough I'd learn to eat things like that and be grateful. She also mentioned that the people of Africa were starving for tomatoes and my Christian duty was to clean up my plate for their sake. She didn't think it was funny when I asked Jackie to put all my tomato hunks in a doggie bag so the missionary could take them back to Africa with her.

I managed to smile through it all and finally wound up pouring the tomato juice into the ashtray to keep it from soaking into my cornbread.

I enjoyed my dinner immensely, but the ladies never did seem to get back in the mood for eating.

In the areas where I am secure, where I know who I am, I never grow angry. In such areas I refuse to let the world—even the world of my wife and my mother—mold me into its image. It is only when I am on shaky ground, unsure of my stance or afraid to take off my mask and let folks see me the way I really am, that I explode in the defense mechanism of anger.

Salvation, in its purest sense, is becoming the person you really are— the person God created you to be. It is there you achieve the individuality and personal identity for which each man yearns.

Occasionally I daydream of being on a life raft at sea, and a case of tomatoes comes floating by. Would I, under such circumstances, eat one? Perhaps one day I shall. In fact, there are times when I wonder, Is this the day?

But until then, I am content with my uniqueness and feel no need to defend my status.

In the meantime, pass the catsup, please.

If You're Ever in Florida

Well, it finally happened. A whole family of total strangers showed up for Sunday breakfast at our house. Actually they weren't total strangers; somewhere I had met them and issued one of those general invitations that you never expect anyone to respond to: "If you're ever in Florida, drop in and see us."

They did.

On a Sunday morning before church, would you believe.

Jackie and I had flown in late the night before. We agreed we'd sleep as late as we could, skip breakfast and get up just in time to get to the meeting house for church services. Everything changed when the phone began ringing incessantly at 7 a.m.

Last year, after women began calling me in the middle of the night and breathing sexily into the phone, Jackie insisted I put the phone on her side of the bed. If it rang in the middle of the night, she would take care of the sexily breathing women in short order. It was a great idea, only she never answered it. Once asleep, she becomes like the tree planted by the waters—she will not be moved. As the phone rang and rang, I crawled over her inert body and fumbled for the receiver.

I'm always afraid I might have lost my voice during the night, so I practice talking before I pick up the receiver.

"Ah...(cough, cough)...hello...(cough, gag, sputter)...hello." Assured I could speak, I finally grabbed the cord on the receiver and pulled it to me, over my slumbering wife and onto my pillow.

"We're here!" a man's chipper voice sang out on the other end of the line. "We've driven all night from Kansas and we're pooped."

I could feel Jackie stiffen as she rapidly came awake. "Who's 'we' and how many of 'we' are there?" she mumbled.

By this time I had my hand over the mouthpiece and was trying to get the cord untangled from her hair-rollers. "Uh, how many do you have with you?" I asked.

He laughed. "The whole family, of course. Don't you remember saying to bring the gang and come on down?"

"Oh, sure," I said with a phony laugh. "Let me give you directions. We can hardly wait."

I hung up and fell back on the pillow. "Who was that?" Jackie demanded, now sitting straight up in bed.

"It wasn't anybody. It was a dream," I mumbled.

"Dream, nothing," she retorted, squirming out of bed and pulling the covers off me. "You just invited someone to our house at seven o'clock and you don't even know who it is. This place is a wreck. We haven't even unpacked our suitcases. You get the kids up and I'll start on the bathrooms.

"And remember, you have a special singing group at church this morning, plus the Gideons and the missionary kids leaving for the Bahamas."

Five minutes later the doorbell was ringing. There they were—all five of them. They hugged us, put the kids to sleep on the front-room sofas and headed for the bathrooms.

I helped Jackie with breakfast while they took showers. "How are we going to learn their names?" she said, as she scrambled through the cupboard for some powdered milk. (We're always out of whole milk when company comes, it seems.)

"I'm going to disappear upstairs and shave," I said. "Since you've never met them, you can introduce yourself to them and get their names. Then when I come back down make a deliberate point of calling their names in front of me."

I started up the stairs and then had a horrible thought. "What if it was you who invited them, not me?" I asked her.

Jackie chased me up the stairs. "My weakness is screaming at the children," she said. "Yours is inviting strangers to drop by if they're in Florida."

She was right, of course. I should have known that sooner or later someone would take that trite phrase of mine seriously.

"Maybe they're relatives," my daughter Robin giggled while I shaved.

"No, relatives don't call first—they just show up. Like Uncle Kenneth did last year with his portable bed he had to sleep on and his blender so he could get up in the middle of the night to make something he had to drink every three hours—made from celery leaves, turnip tops and parsley—called 'the Green Drink.' No, these folks aren't relatives. We don't have any relatives in Kansas."

"Maybe they're Bonnie and Clyde," Bruce said, his eyes round with excitement.

They weren't. In fact, after Jackie called on the man to ask the blessing at breakfast, I actually remembered where I had met them. Of course, we still didn't know their last names, but my enterprising wife had an answer for that, too. She got them to sign the guest book—just to make sure they weren't angels unawares.

After church our new friends drove on to Miami. This time, though, it was my wife who waved them on their way saying, "Be sure and stop by when you head back for Kansas."

So, if you're ever in Florida—honk as you drive past our town.

Sometimes It Just Doesn't Pay to Explain

I'm having a hard time enjoying my Filipino houseguest. Already his presence has upset my way of living—a way in which I have grown very comfortable. The alternatives are not pleasant: either get rid of him or change my way of living.

I met Aley Gonzalez three years before on my first visit to Mindanao, the southernmost island of the archipelago. An ex-boxer with more than a hundred professional fights under his bantamweight belt, this middle-aged, tough-as-coconut-husk, brown-skinned Filipino was preaching like he fought in the ring—both hands jabbing, feet dancing and always boring in for the knockout punch. With the aid of a vintage motorcycle and motorized outrigger canoe, he would go into some of the most inaccessible places in the island chain, starting churches and training pastors.

His average salary was fifty pesos a month (about seven dollars) and his entire wardrobe consisted of three pairs of pants, some shirts, a cheap nylon jacket and a pair of rubber slaps called "flip-flops."

Few Americans ever visit his out-of-the-way location in the province of Agusan del Norte. To get there you go seven hundred miles south from Manila, cross two volcanos, pass through the straits at Mactan, and take a jeep ride through the rain forests to the coastal barrio of Cabadbaran. Those of us who had visited there had encouraged Aley to visit the States. It would surely broaden his perspective and make him a better preacher. Or so we thought.

Then Aley arrived at my Florida home. My son Tim had worked that summer and saved money for an expensive new slalom water-ski. Knowing how much Aley loved the water (we had spent some happy hours swimming together in the China Sea), I took him with us for a late afternoon ride in our new boat.

On the way to the marina we passed a golf course.

"What are those men doing out there in the pasture, all dressed up? Are they getting ready to have a big evangelistic meeting?"

Aley, it seems, relates everything to the gospel. I explained to him that, although they were dressed up like peacocks, they weren't going to church. They were playing a game.

"Why do they hit that little ball with those sticks?" he asked. "Does somebody hire them to do that?"

I started to give him an explanation but realized it would sound foolish, so I stopped. "We have a lot of people in America who do odd things," I mumbled.

Aley nodded. He seemed to understand.

"We hear in the Philippines there are many Americans without work. When jobs become more plentiful they will probably stop this foolishness."

I didn't have the heart to tell him that only the rich could afford to be fools.

Aley was impressed with my boat.

"It is very expensive," he said softly, running his hands along the sleek fiberglass deck. "It must have cost twenty thousand pesos. But what do you use it for? Do your sons and daughters fish for a living?"

He could tell I was having trouble with an answer.

"Perhaps you and your wife go up and down the river and preach the gospel to all those out-of-work people swinging their sticks at the balls?" he asked, knowing that somewhere I had hidden a sensible answer.

When I explained we used the boat only to pull water-skiers and for some sport-fishing, he was startled. I could tell he was thinking of the thirty-two miles he had to paddle his outrigger just to get to the small village of San Jose where he preached the gospel. And here I was with this sleek red-and-white fiberglass beauty. He turned his eyes away and said nothing.

Coming back we stopped at the home of a friend who has three motorcycles in the garage. Aley's eyes danced with excitement, thinking of his battered old Kawasaki.

"These people must go many places helping the poor, feeding the hungry and preaching the gospel," he said approvingly.

When I explained that although these people belonged to the church they weren't active Christians, he was startled. "You have church members who do not preach? How can this be? The Bible says all church members should be preaching the gospel. What then do they use these motorcycles for?"

I explained they were dirt bikes, used only to roar around the woods, going no place. I saw that same pensive look move across his face like clouds over the sun. "There are many things about America which I

159

need to learn,'' he said, amazed.

I drove home a different way. I didn't want him to see the yachts on the river, the dune buggies in the driveways or the imposing church buildings which sit idle except for a few feeble groans on Sunday morning. I didn't want to face any more of his questions. It was the same feeling I had many years ago when, as a young idealist, I attended a church service when they dedicated a $75,000 stained-glass window—to the glory of God.

But I have mellowed since then. (A state which I imagine Aley would describe as one step removed from going rotten.)

Aley was too kind to say anything to me. But last night I couldn't help but see the expression on his face when he looked in my closet and saw all those shoes.

I haven't been sleeping well recently.

NINE

Growing Up the Hard Way

The Great Pea Story

Long years ago, before I learned you cannot run a family the way you run a military school, we used to have in our house something I called the Buckingham Demerit System. In this ingenious system each of the five children was assigned certain chores around the house. Failure to perform the duties resulted in points marked off on a big wall poster. Successfully performed duties were rewarded with stars. At the end of each week stars and demerits were totaled. Those who came out on top received rewards. Those on bottom, various punishments.

Napoleon, I had been told, ran his entire army on just such a system—handing out medals and exacting punishment.

The Russians use it in their factories—hanging up pictures of the worker of the week and publicly humiliating those who don't make their quota.

Beginning at West Point and extending throughout the armed forces, military personnel are motivated by the promise of reward and the threat of punishment.

School children are graded with good and bad marks on report cards.

If such a system was good enough for the great American military and educational institutions, surely it would work in the Buckingham house as well, I assumed.

As usual, my assumptions failed to take into account the people involved. In this case, my five children.

At first the kids were excited about the system. They loved the idea of getting rewards, and equally (perhaps even more) loved seeing their brothers and sisters getting demerits on the big poster on the kitchen wall.

Duties included such things as making your bed, emptying trash cans, clearing the table, washing and drying dishes, sweeping the carport, brushing your teeth, and so forth. At the top of the list of things to do—and the thing which carried the greatest number of demerits if not done—was eating everything on your plate.

Like many small-town American children, I grew up in a God-fearing, Bible-believing home where my father prayed before every meal and my mother quoted Scripture when we were done. The only verse she seemed to know, however, was a passage from Leviticus that said, "Thou shalt eat everything on thy plate." In fact, in our home leaving food on your plate ranked right along with taking the Lord's name in vain as a horrible sin.

I can remember my mother, when I would sit there staring at my oatmeal, reminding me of the starving children in Africa. One Saturday morning I got up from the breakfast table and walked back into the kitchen carrying my oatmeal dish. I had decided to make the ultimate sacrifice and was going to give my oatmeal to the starving Africans. All she had to do was mail it to them. She rewarded my sacrificial attitude by sending me to my room instead of letting me go out to play.

Although I never understood this emphasis on eating everything on your plate, it seemed so right, so pure, so holy that I've always insisted my children do the same thing.

On a particular dark and stormy night Jackie had to leave the dinner table early to attend a class meeting of some sort. She left behind four of the five children. The youngest, Sandy, was spending the night with friends. Unfortunately, Jackie also left behind four plates on the table— each heaped with a generous serving of something not a single one of the children liked to eat: large, green English peas. The children dubbed them "rolling ball peas," as opposed to the smaller variety of peas which didn't roll but stuck together. The peas were still piled on each plate, untouched, when Jackie excused herself from the table and rushed out the front door.

"Be sure and stick to your guns," she said over her shoulder. "Don't let the kids con you out of having to eat their peas."

"Yeah," our twelve-year-old son, Bruce, muttered. "I'll bet the Africans would walk on fire just to eat them."

I assured my wife that I, who made the laws, was quite capable of enforcing them. No house full of little kids could face me down on something as important as eating their peas.

Returning to the table I was met by four scowling faces, each of them looking at me over an untouched pile of green peas. "Daddy, you know we don't like rolling ball peas," ten-year-old Robin complained. "Can't you let us off just this one time?"

Feeling the wisdom of Solomon falling on me like a mantle, I answered sagely, "No, Honey. But I'll make an arrangement with you. If you eat your peas, I'll wash the dishes."

More scowls. "You were going to wash the dishes anyway," Bruce said.

Maybe Solomon wasn't the one to choose as a model father. After all, it was his sons who divided the kingdom and tried to kill each other.

I resorted to force. "If you don't eat your peas, you can go straight to bed."

Tim, age seven, took one more look at the mountain of green balls on his plate and got up and left the room—head down, bottom lip poked out. In a moment he was back with his pajamas on.

He tried once more. "Do I have to eat them all?"

"All!" I replied sternly. He took another look and with a sigh of resignation said, "Then good night, Daddy." He was gone.

I got up and started on the dishes, hoping to inspire the rest of them. Moments later Robin announced she was through. She handed me her clean plate and hastily left the room. I'm not normally suspicious of my ten-year-old daughter, but something prodded me to follow her down the hall. I found her in the bathroom with an empty napkin in her hand. Peering into the toilet, I saw—floating like an armada arrayed for sea battle—a flotilla of green peas.

Robin was assigned to bed, also.

Back in the kitchen the contest was gaining momentum. Bruce had counted his peas and found he had six more than his nine-year-old sister, Bonnie. I ruled he could leave six peas on his plate.

I returned to the kitchen sink and in a moment I heard a great coughing and gagging from Bonnie, accompanied by Bruce's wild laughter.

I rushed to the table and pounded her on the back. She was close to strangling. I shouted for an explanation. Bruce quit laughing long enough to explain that Bonnie was trying to swallow her peas one at a time—whole—so she wouldn't have to chew them up. One had gone down the wrong way.

"Here," said Bruce, "let me show you how to do it." With that he placed a pea on the back of his tongue, like a capsule, and gulped it down with milk.

"AGHHHHH!" he choked, spraying milk all over the table. The pesky pea dislodged and flew across the table into Bonnie's plate—where it nested anonymously among its brethren.

Bonnie screamed. Now she couldn't eat her peas because she didn't know which one Bruce had spit in her plate. I was about to suggest that Bruce divide his peas with her when he spilled his milk. Most of his peas floated over the edge of his plate onto the floor and began their natural flow toward Africa.

I gave up. Shooing them away from the table, I went back and got Tim and Robin out of bed. No sense in punishing them when the others got away scot-free for the same crime.

The kids watched television while I finished up in the kitchen. Somehow those four little connivers had not only conned me into cleaning up the kitchen but had completed supper without eating a single pea.

When Jackie came home later, the children were safely tucked in bed, prayers had been said, and I was reading peacefully in the den.

"What's that big poster board rolled up in the garbage can?" Jackie asked as she came in through the carport entrance.

"That's the Buckingham Demerit System poster," I said.

"What happened?"

"For the sake of our relationship it's better if I don't go into it."

"You mean the program is over and we can now get back to normal?"

"If 'normal' is what I experienced tonight, we're already back."

Pomp and Circumstances

There is something special about a high school graduation ceremony held outside. Especially when it rains.

My problems started earlier in the evening. Since it was my oldest son's graduation night, we took the entire family out to eat. I parked the car near the highway. We had just finished ordering from the menu when a man seated next to the plate glass window stood up and said in a loud voice so all in the restaurant could hear, "The owner of a brown station wagon better get outside. Somebody just clobbered his car."

I waved goodbye to my food and spent the next forty-five minutes talking with police and a scared young woman who had neither driver's license nor insurance—yet had managed to jump the curb, skid through the parking lot and smash my car. I kept thinking, of the five people who have run into my car over the years, none of them has had insurance.

We arrived at the high school football stadium and found a choice parking place a quarter of a mile from the gate. Of course, by then it had started to sprinkle. Jackie squeezed my clenched fist and said, "Remember last week how you told all those people in church they should praise God for all things. What a wonderful opportunity to put your preaching into practice."

All I could reply was "Grrrr!"

At precisely three minutes before eight (graduation was to begin precisely at eight) the sprinkle stopped—and became a downpour. The high school band, which had already taken its place on the field, now provided the evening's entertainment by rushing around gathering up meltable things like kettle drums and sheet music and stuffing them in the back of a panel truck.

Of course, those of us wedged in the grandstands didn't have a panel truck, so we just sat it out in miserable silence. As the rain got harder, miracles began taking place. From nowhere people produced raincoats and umbrellas. Hundreds of them appeared.

Through the side of her mouth Jackie reminded me that she had suggested we bring umbrellas, but I had told her real men don't carry umbrellas—they have faith.

My faith was the magnitude of a paper program about the size of a folded-up handkerchief. Unfortunately, we only had one of these. (Jackie reminded me, out of the side of her mouth again, that I had been in too much of a hurry to pick up one for her so she was graciously going to use mine to cover her head.)

I considered leaving, but there was no way to do it without losing both eyes and an eardrum on all those sharp spines that were sticking out from the umbrellas that had miraculously appeared. So I sat. And endured.

To make matters worse I discovered I was under the drip from the umbrellas in front of me and behind me. Not only was I getting my own rain, I was getting their rain, too—down my back and in my lap.

I had the strongest urge to stand up and shout: "All intelligent people get up and leave. Only fools remain."

I didn't, of course. I just sat still with the other fools.

An hour later the rain went away. The band reappeared. (Most of them, it seems, had been in the back of the panel truck with the kettle drums.) "Pomp and Circumstance" was sounded, and some place in that sloshing mob of indistinguishable, gowned figures plodding their way through the mud was my eldest son—the pride and joy of my life.

I never did get to see him.

"Your son only graduates once," Jackie said, squeezing my hand as tears mixed with the water dripping out of her hair.

"Only by faith do I know he is down there," I replied.

"Look how much you have to be thankful for," Jackie smiled sweetly. "You still have four more to go."

I nodded. And sneezed. I can hardly wait.

Everything I Need to Know
I Learned Before I Could Shave

Everyone needs to learn at least one major truth a year. Hopefully, two. But I figure if you learn at least one new thing a year—I mean really learn it—you'll be so far ahead of the pack you'll not have to worry about ever being overtaken.

The older we dogs grow, I've discovered, the harder it is for us to learn new tricks. Wineskins have the same problem. Keeping mine flexible is increasingly difficult—and painful.

Once you become an adult, most lessons are learned through the pain of failure. That's the way the kingdom operates.

The truth, Jesus said, will make you free. But first it makes you miserable.

It's like the little sign I have on the wall of my study: "Whom God loves He shakes the hell out of."

Fortunate is the person who fails early in adulthood. Late failures can be fatal.

Children, on the other hand, learn quickly with a minimum of pain. In fact, as I look back, my best lessons were learned before I started to shave.

I learned how important it was to share my toys. I learned if I left my toys out in the rain they rusted and didn't work. I learned to say, "I'm sorry," when I lost my temper and beat up my little brother. I learned if I sassed my mother my daddy would hurt my bottom.

Many of today's crop of young adults never learned these lessons. It's tough to learn when you're twenty-eight—especially if you have a wife and two children and are living on the financial edge—that if you leave your vacuum cleaner out in the rain after you've cleaned your car it will be ruined.

There were other important things I learned. Don't pick your nose in public. Don't put money in your mouth. Eat vegetables. Don't tinkle on the toilet seat. Rainbows always follow the rain and every night has a sunrise.

I learned it was good to laugh and sing. No meal should ever be eaten—anywhere—without thanking God for food. And never go to sleep until you've asked Jesus to watch over you and give you sweet dreams.

During my years at summer camp, I learned no matter how good a swimmer I thought I was, never to go in the water without a buddy. I learned to line up my shoes in pairs under my cot and tuck the shoestrings inside because I never knew when my cabin might be inspected. I learned never to play ping-pong with a kid who carried his own set of paddles and never to put a live turtle in my counselor's bed until

I was sure the turtle had already gone to the bathroom.

No later than the third grade I learned I would never be the best. In every class, on every team, there was always someone better than I was. I'm thankful for a dad who never punished me for a bad grade as long as he was convinced I had done my best—but always punished me for bad behavior.

I learned some other things from my dad. He taught me always to look a man in the eye when I shook his hand, that a man's word should be his bond, and that a real man loves his wife forever.

In the fourth grade, when a cruel teacher humiliated me in front of the class for something I hadn't done, I learned I was a fool to expect this world to give me a fair shake. It was a hard lesson for I wanted to believe everyone was like my dad—good, fair and just. When that same teacher, three weeks later, made fun of the little girl in the next aisle because she wet her panties in class, I knew from then on not to expect justice or kindness from the world. It's not that I don't get upset when I'm cheated, slandered, ignored, misunderstood or used—and then cast out. But at least I know what to expect.

When a kid stops whining, "But it isn't fair," and realizes this is an unjust world, he has matured.

Maturity also means you've learned that even though the used-car dealer has a dove on his sign you should still have at least one other mechanic check the transmission before you buy the car.

The summer between grades six and seven I got my first job—working for my dad's grizzled old crew foreman picking late-bloom citrus. Even though I was the owner's son, he fired me the second week on the job. But the lessons learned were invaluable. I learned I only got paid if I worked. I also learned if I mouthed off to my boss that there were a lot of people out there who needed work and were itching to take my place.

What a great lesson! Today I work with people who say they don't have to submit to authority because they are "King's Kids." They answer only to God. Others don't work because they have "faith" to believe God will send along some rich man who will give them money. They don't understand that the reason rich people are rich is they never give their money to spoiled kids or deadbeats. I'm grateful that nearly everything I own I've had to work for.

Now having just entered the second half of my fifth decade, I pause, reflect and give thanks for lessons learned early in life—lessons a lot of folks seemed to have missed, or they have forgotten.

What a wonderful world it would be if we all did the things we learned as kids. Give each other cookies and milk when we skin our knees. Always hold hands when you cross the street. Never go into deep water without a buddy. Say you're sorry, even when you're not to blame. Laugh and sing a lot. Don't tinkle where someone else has to sit. Never get into bed—any bed—without asking God to look out for you. And remember, no matter how dark the night, God always brings the dawn.

Spiritual Maturity

Everyone, it seems, is talking about spiritual maturity. This morning I received three new books in the mail. One was on the spiritually mature man, another on the spiritually mature church and a third on raising spiritually mature kids.

I love the term. It has a good ring to it—even if no one has any idea what it means.

Last night at our home group meeting, someone mentioned a certain well-known speaker.

"Ahhh," one woman sighed, "he's spiritually mature."

I think that means nobody can understand him.

People, I've discovered, don't like to have their spiritual maturity questioned. They don't even like it when I ask, "What is spiritual maturity, anyway?"

They snarl, "The *really* spiritually mature man would never ask a question like that."

Last Saturday, however, I got an answer to my question.

All summer my oldest son, Bruce, has been taking flying lessons. Saturday morning he passed his flight exam and received his private ticket, meaning he's qualified to carry passengers in his rented plane. He called me from the airport and asked if I wanted to go for a ride with him. The rest of the family, excited, piled in the car with me. They wanted to see this great event.

Bruce taxied the little Cessna 150 up to the front of the private terminal and shut down the engine. I walked out on the tarmac and squeezed into the right-hand seat of the two-seat, single-engine plane.

It was broiling hot as I waited in the cockpit for him to complete his preflight checklist before restarting the engine.

Memories, hundreds of them, flooded through my mind. I remembered my first flight after I completed my private exam—twenty years before. That time Bruce was my first passenger, strapped tightly in the seat beside me in the ancient Piper J-4. His little blond head obscured behind the rattling, vibrating old instrument panel, he could barely peer out the side window.

There were other memories: flying off dirt airstrips...getting lost on cross-country flights and having to fly at treetop level so I could read the names of the towns on the water towers...being on top of the clouds and praying desperately for a hole...spending all those hours over the Amazon jungle when I was writing my book on jungle pilots....

It had been almost two years since I had been at the controls of a small plane. When I sold my last plane I suspected I would never own another. It was just too expensive—and too time-consuming.

Now I was sitting beside my eldest son as he began his own flying career. It was a proud moment.

Bruce completed his preflight check, tediously pointing his finger at every instrument, checking the controls, making sure my seat belt was fastened and my door closed and locked.

"Clear!" he shouted at no one as he twisted the key in the magneto switch and punched the starter button.

But nothing happened.

Either the battery was low or the starter was stuck.

He wiggled the key, shouted, "Clear!" again and pushed the button. The only sound was a small click under the cowling.

He tried several times, then looked at me apologetically. Helplessly.

I knew how he felt. His mother and sisters were behind the chain link fence, watching. Several grizzled old pilots were standing around the apron, waiting to see what was going to happen.

"The planes I flew didn't have starters," I grinned. "Let me show you how the old-timers cranked up."

"What are you going to do?" he asked.

"Just make sure all your switches are off," I commanded.

I stepped to the front of the plane and took the metal prop in my hands, pulled it through a couple of times, then shouted: "Turn on the master switch, crack the throttle, and whatever you do—keep your feet on the brakes."

A big breath. Hands on the prop. Pull down. Jump back. And the engine roared to life.

Bruce was impressed as I climbed back into the cockpit, my hair blowing in the backwash.

All the old urges were taking over. Suddenly I was a pilot again. I could hardly keep my hands off the controls.

Bruce picked up the radio mike and called ground control.

"Taxi to runway thirteen and hold," the voice came back through the speaker.

"Where's thirteen?" Bruce said to me.

I realized he was unfamiliar with the airport. I automatically put my feet on the rudders and reached for the throttle. "I'll taxi out for you," I said paternally.

My son gently pushed my hand from the throttle, picked up the microphone and once again called ground control.

"I'm unfamiliar with the airport," he said. "Can you direct me to runway thirteen?"

The overhead speaker crackled to life as the man in the tower gave exact directions.

I sat back. The flight belonged to Bruce, not me.

As we took off and Bruce waggled his wings at his mom and his sisters waving below, I realized he had many years of safe flying ahead. He had exhibited the three qualities necessary to stay alive.

He recognized his limitations and had a teachable spirit.

He was not afraid to ask for help when he needed it.

He was not afraid to exert authority—even over his dad when necessary.

Both of us learned something about spiritual maturity that day.

Pack Rats in the Kingdom

A wise man once suggested we should take inventory every two months and discard everything not used during that period of time. It's a valid spiritual principle. God seems to be telling His people to travel light, not burdened by things of this world.

But what do you do when you have a whole room full of things that might come in handy one day?

About every two years I'm forced to clean out the back room of our house, which is tantamount to going through the Smithsonian Institution and deciding what to keep and what to throw away. Our back room—which we affectionately call the "junk room"—is part utility, part workshop and part storage hole. It usually takes about two years for the junk to begin to take over the living area of our house. It spreads slowly, like crabgrass, encroaching first into the den, then into the kitchen and finally onto the dining room table. If we didn't do something, we would eventually have to move out of the house.

Every so often, then, I declare "operation throwaway."

But what do you do with odds and ends that you never have used—but just might?

• A mayonnaise jar filled with assorted keys. I know, they don't fit any lock in the house, but you never can tell....

• Three electric train sets. True, all the tracks are different gauges and the transformers are burned out. But one of these days electric trains will be antiques and perhaps my children would like to show them to their children. (No doubt so they could put them in their junk room.)

• Christmas candles: various sizes and colors—about half of which are broken.

• Screws, washers, nuts, bolts: some of which have exotic looks to them and obviously would be impossible to replace—if you knew where they fit.

• Assortments of ballpoint and felt-tipped pens: none of which writes anymore and all of which are jammed in the pencil holder next to the telephone along with the screws, washers, nuts, bolts—and a pink-headed diaper pin that has not been used in twenty-five years.

Then there are the old Christmas cards. Jackie heard someplace that nursing homes take these, cut them up, lacquer them and lace them together into little baskets and dishes to hold things like screws, washers, nuts, bolts, diaper pins and old keys. You can also use them to store old Christmas cards. We've been saving them for years but never have found a nursing home that's doing this.

From surplus sales I've acquired lots of camping gear: aluminum cooking sets, cartons of Sterno canned heat, water purifiers and salt pills. All so far unused. I keep thinking I'll use this stuff as I did when I was a Boy Scout, but every time we go camping this stuff stays home.

In an upstairs cedar closet I have a marvelous collection of GI pants, the ones with the big pockets on the sides to hold spare hand grenades. I once bought six pairs during a closeout sale. All are too small now, but I keep telling myself that one day there'll be no more war and they won't make swell pants like these anymore. Besides, I can always use them on camping trips in case I want to take along the water purifiers, salt pills, cooking sets and canned heat. In the meantime, I had better hold onto them.

I never wear a hat, but you never can tell when....

Maybe someday I might play that old concertina again.

And everybody saves *National Geographics*, don't they?

I'll bet my son can hardly wait to get his hands on a beer mug inscribed "ATO, Mercer University, 1954."

And a man never knows when he might need a broken phonograph and a big, long cardboard box filled with bent curtain rods.

It's like the old clothes in my closet. I just can't bear to throw them away. I know the style has changed since the '50s, but they are still perfectly good. The zippers work, the cloth will last for another fifty years, and despite the fact no one wears zoot suits anymore, you never can tell....

The same is true of wide ties. When the styles changed twenty years ago I decided this time I wasn't going to get caught napping. I knew that, sooner or later, wide ties would make a comeback. So I stored them away—more than a hundred of them. Some are made out of carpet cloth, others have handpainted Hawaiian girls on the front. But all are perfectly good and you never can tell....

Then there's the survival food that fills an entire closet in the guest bedroom. We bought it during the "great tribulation scare" several years ago when all those prophecies were going around that Christians should buy a year's supply of emergency food. At last inventory we had seventeen restaurant-sized cans of soybeans packed in nitrogen; fourteen cans of hard, red wheat grain (we also bought a huge, hand-cranked wheat grain grinder); twenty-five cans of dried beans; and twelve cans of dried barley. Under both beds in the guest bedroom are dozens of cases of things like whole-wheat pasta elbows, cheddar cheese powder, oat flakes, something called triticale flakes and an even dozen cans of bulghur-soy grits.

"You bought this stuff to see us through the great tribulation," Jackie moaned, "but just preparing and eating it would be an even greater tribulation."

Yet you never can tell....

I remember reading about a man who never threw anything away. He stored it all in his attic and one day, you guessed it, his house collapsed on top of him.

Jackie reminded me that last summer we took a long vacation and lived happily out of one suitcase for almost six weeks. If I could get along without that old commando machete and those five pairs of holey tennis shorts then, I could surely get along without them now.

"The best thing that could happen to us would be to have to move overseas, or to have a fire," Jackie lamented.

A friend stopped by one evening and asked why our entire family was sitting out on the front steps.

"The house finally filled up," Jackie said. "The only place left to sit down is on the toilet in the upstairs bathroom and Grandma's in there now."

"We go through our house twice a year," our friend said piously. "Everything we haven't used in two months we throw away."

I winced with pain. But that evening, just to get to my chair in the den, I made a decision. I made everyone in the family throw away something. My daughter threw away my old ammunition belt. I threw away the kids' three electric trains. My son threw away his sister's trash can full of mismatched hair curlers, and Jackie threw away my 1954 cracked beer mug.

Later, sitting quietly in the den, I heard a terrible commotion in the junk room. Opening the door, I saw my two teenage children carting stuff from the garbage bin back into the house.

"Gosh, Dad," my son said with a look of dismay on his face, "one day these old electric trains will be antiques." I closed the door and returned to the television. Like father, like son. I have bred another generation of pack rats.

An eighty-five-year-old woman wrote saying, "I've been one of those persons who never goes anywhere without a thermometer, a hot water bottle, a raincoat and a parachute. If I had to do it again, I'd travel lighter."

Me too. But once you're loaded down, it's almost impossible to unload.

That's the trouble with us pack rats. We hate to get rid of anything.

Watch and Pray

When I was a kid the one thing I wanted more than anything else was a wristwatch.

My dad was a pocketwatch man. As long as I can remember he carried one of those round, stainless steel watches.

The only men I knew who wore wristwatches were the rich, the famous, those who didn't work outside, and flashy men who appeared in magazine ads. No wonder I wanted a wristwatch.

The Christmas before I graduated from high school, my parents gave me a Mido wristwatch. They felt I needed it when I went off to college.

Back then Mido was top of the line. They had just come out with a self-winding mechanism, meaning as long as the watch was in motion it didn't need winding.

I wore the watch for twenty-five years. It kept perfect time. But as I grew older I began to look around at the flashy gold watches worn by the big-time preachers. Envious, I determined that sooner or later, I'd move up.

In 1972 I made my first trip to South America. My thirteen-year-old son, Bruce, accompanied me. We were scheduled for a week in Bogota, then another week visiting missionaries in the Amazon valley. Our last day in the city was spent sightseeing. That evening, heading back to the hotel, we were stopped by a seedy-looking fellow on the sidewalk who whispered, "Hey, gringo, wanna' buy a watch?"

He pulled up his coat sleeve, and there was the most beautiful gold Omega I had ever seen. I knew my chance had come. "Watch me, Bruce," I smiled wisely, "and learn."

Turning to the watch salesman I asked, "How much?"

He glanced in all directions, then pulled me over to the side of a building. "Three hundred pesos, senor," he said. "I must sell. My sister needs medicine."

Worldly wise, I shook my head. "Too much! I give you fifty pesos."

We haggled. He explained what a bargain I was getting. The watch was a genuine Swiss Omega. Solid gold. He shook it so I could hear the self-winding mechanism. It even said "automatico" on the face.

At the time it never occurred to me to ask why a Swiss watch would have Spanish writing on the face. All I could see was the sun reflecting off the gold band. We finally settled on one hundred pesos—worth at that time about fifteen dollars.

"These guys will really take you if you're not tough," I told Bruce as we entered the hotel, handing him my Mido.

Three days later, visiting our missionary friends in the jungle, I noticed my new watch had stopped. Not only that, my wrist was turning green. That night in the dining hall I mentioned it to the missions director.

"Is it a gold Omega that says 'automatico'?" he asked.

I knew I was in trouble.

"Hey, everyone," the director shouted to the group, "guess who got suckered!"

That night my son returned my Mido. He knew better than to laugh.

When I got back home I sheepishly took my "Omega" to the watchmaker. When he opened the back a tiny piece of razorblade fell out. "What's that?" I asked.

"That's the 'automatic' mechanism," he laughed. "It slides back and forth. The watch is worthless."

I wore my Mido for another ten years, shedding it briefly for a stainless steel Seiko I had purchased in Hong Kong, which I finally gave away.

Then, last year, my publisher returned from Korea. In an editorial meeting he presented me with a solid gold Rolex. "Now you can look like all the big-time evangelists," he said.

I was overwhelmed.

Three weeks later, while preaching in Dallas, I glanced at my watch. I was horrified. The second hand was moving counterclockwise. When I took it to a jeweler, he looked and laughed. "With a true Rolex the second hand goes clockwise. Also, it sweeps, rather than clicking off the seconds. This watch is worthless."

"What do you mean, worthless?" my publisher howled when I confronted him. "I paid a street vendor thirty dollars."

I went back to my Mido.

Then, six months ago, everything changed. I was having lunch with a Jewish friend who deals in discount everythings. He was showing me his gold Rolex.

"Yeah!" I laughed. "I used to have one just like it. It started running backwards."

"Not like this one," he said seriously. I kept on laughing until I saw the second hand, sweeping smoothly around the face.

"What's it worth?" I asked, now sober.

He held up seven fingers. "This one's gold-filled," he said. "The solid gold models are worth ten grand or more."

Then, suddenly, in a moment of grateful generosity, he pulled it off his wrist and handed it to me. "We Jews aren't known for this," he laughed, "but I want you to have it."

"I can't afford it," I moaned. "I'll have to buy a new car to go with it."

"Do you know why God gave you a $7,000 watch?" my wife asked that night. "To keep you from making fun of all the big-time preachers."

I didn't sleep well. Twenty years ago my world centered around owning an expensive gold watch. Now I had one and didn't want it. Why should I own something that expensive when others had nothing?

"Maybe God wants you to give it to someone else," Jackie suggested.

I wished she hadn't said that. I didn't sleep well that night either. Should I give it away or not?

Not won out. I enjoyed flashing it. Especially at preachers' meetings.

In June, when I went overseas, I was afraid to take the watch. I left it at home in a safe place. When I returned it had stopped running. Jackie took it to the jeweler for me and returned, laughing. "It's a fake," she giggled. "Outside it's Rolex. Inside it's Sears & Roebuck."

I was relieved—but sad. My friend who gave it to me knew it was a fake all along. But I didn't. I only wish I had given it away when I thought it was worth $7,000. Now all I had was another worthless watch—and no blessing.

I also have a thirty-nine-year-old Mido which keeps perfect time. What else is a watch supposed to do?

Measuring the Spiritual Giants

There's a lot of talk these days about "spiritual giants." Pick up the publicity brochure from any of a dozen or so "Jesus" rallies around the nation and you'll see the same pictures in all of them. These are the modern "spiritual giants." Dressed in seven-league boots, they stride from the Gulf to the Great Lakes, march from the rolling hills of Pennsylvania to the sunny climes of California—spreading the gospel in word and song.

They are a necessary breed—these spiritual giants. And despite their sometimes rhinestone-like behavior, they seem to bless a lot of people.

They used to go electronic, appearing on our TV screens. That was in the days before the giant-killing epidemic swept through the electronic world. Dressed in powder blue with carefully sprayed hair, these electronic giants interviewed people who had been delivered from drugs or witchcraft, or those with exciting careers such as putting their heads into lions' mouths. Those days, hopefully, are nearly past.

But never fear, spiritual giants always have a way of rising above the common folk in order to be noticed.

Spiritual giants distribute cassette tapes by the millions. These are mixed blessings as they rain down upon us as the hail on Egypt. To some these tapes are the bread of salvation, their only hope of surviving in this dry, thirsty desert of humanism. To others they are the false prophets of the day, leading people up every conceivable (and some inconceivable) path of deception.

You name it, and your friendly spiritual giant will have it catalogued in his tape library: Faith, End Times, Prosperity, Angel Visitations—even the secrets of the pyramids. Recently Pat Wells, a Tennessee doctor's wife, sent me a tape containing the croaking of four thousand frogs from all the swamps of the world. She thought it would be good to use as background while I preached my sermon on "Frogs, Princes and Watch-Out-for-Warts."

Spiritual giants also write books and magazine columns, and they autograph their wares at the annual Giant Conventions sponsored by the bookseller and broadcasting associations. There these spiritual heavyweights stride slowly down the aisles much as huge sharks glide through the thousands of other fish in a tank at a seaquarium. They

178

seem unperturbed by the booths containing Jesus T-shirts for your dog, press-on rhinestone crosses for the seat and knees of blue jeans, and other stuff known affectionately as "Jesus Junk."

As speakers, most giants are very busy—booked far into the future. Many have their own agents, using such well-known West Coast firms as Spiritual Giants, Inc.; Hulks for Him; or Amazing Amazons (for female giants).

But I have a problem. As much as I detest giantism, deep inside I really yearn to be one. As a result, I sometimes speak at Jesus rallies, wear powder blue on TV (no hair spray, however—it makes the flies stick to my bald head), and write books and columns. And I have, in the past, even joined the moneychangers at the conventions. Even though I try to be humble, inside there is a barely controlled voice that wants to say to all my fans, "Rise, subjects—your master bids you go and sell his books."

Giants, you see, not only have big heads—they have big feet. They use them to stomp all over those closest to them. As you may know, giants are notoriously clumsy—and sometimes quite ponderous. Therefore, even though a man may have an *enormous* prayer life, possess an *immense* missionary vision, be a *colossal* teacher, demand a *huge* honorarium or even be a *prodigious* writer—he may best be remembered by those near him as a lumbering, insensitive hulk.

All this came to mind as I thought of the introduction given me a while back when I spoke to an audience in Tulsa. My old friend, Bill Sanders, introduced me as his "favorite spiritual giant." Though I wanted genuinely to be humble, I loved the sound of it. Even after I boarded the plane on the way home, I sat there savoring the sweet sound of the words.

I chatted briefly with the woman sitting next to me on the plane and then buried myself in a book. Unlike the apostle Paul, who never quite made it, I had finally arrived at my rightful place in the kingdom. After we were airborne, I felt a tap on my arm. The woman next to me handed me a note.

"Dear Spiritual Leader: I need your advice. I know a lady whose husband had been gone from home for five days and when he came back he wouldn't even talk to his wife. He just sits and reads books. At night he reads books. Sometimes he even goes in the bathroom and reads to keep from talking with his wife. What advice should I give my friend? Can you help?''

I hastily penned an answer.

"Dear Beautiful Woman: Tell her she has three choices. 1) Find a handsome man and talk to him. 2) Go to sleep and hope her bum of a husband will be finished reading when she wakes up. 3) Kick the big dope in the leg and make him talk. Your Friendly Spiritual Giant.''

The woman next to me—my wife for more than thirty years—read the note and kicked me sharply in the shin.

The problem, you see, is that we equate spiritual greatness with big-shotism. And that's sad. Press releases and flowery introductions are a poor shield against the fiery darts of the enemy. Praise God for shepherd boys (and wives) who keep on picking up smooth stones of truth to slay the giants of ego who still inhabit the land.

Camels are not the only ones who have problems getting through the eye of the needle on the way to heaven—so do giants.

Games Men Play

Middle-aged men, more than any other creatures on earth (even middle-aged women), strive to hold on to their youth. Women just don't understand this. Most are too busy applying no-wrinkle cream to comprehend the agony men go through as they approach "the hill" over which all eventually go.

You can fool people only so long with cosmetics: hair dyes, toupees, even plastic surgery. Eventually the aging process will catch up with you. The only sure way to maintain health, the experts say, is by diet and exercise. And exercise means racquetball.

I started playing racquetball the same year I started losing weight. My game has remained about the same: I can beat most of the older fellows—and lose to most of the younger ones. Despite my inability to improve as an athlete, however, racquetball has taught me some valuable lessons about life.

*Lesson 1: Never Play With Anyone Who Used to Play College Football—*especially a lineman.

For several years my primary partner was fellow pastor Curry Vaughan, who had not only played first string guard at West Point but was ten years my junior. He had biceps like Godzilla and went after every shot as if he were charging downfield on a kickoff to smash a helpless midshipman into a pulp. He was the kind of fellow who would laugh after hitting me in the small of the back with a ball going 200 mph—then brag about it for the next three weeks. He finally got close enough to open my head with his racquet. Instead of insisting I go to the emergency room, Curry, a Vietnam veteran, fashioned a quasi-tourniquet out of sweatbands. We went ahead and finished the game, even though we had to stop four times to wipe my blood off the floor so we wouldn't slip. That encounter cost me ten stitches in my forehead. Even though I loved the guy, I felt I had gained an extension on life when he moved to another church. After all, the reason I was playing was to maintain my health—and playing with Curry meant that not only the end of my health, but the end of my life, was always one swing away.

Lesson 2: Never Trust a Left-Hander—at least not on the racquetball court.

Discovery number two came a year later on my way home from the emergency room of the hospital when I determined a twenty-by-forty court is too small to contain four middle-aged men swinging clubs at a wildly bouncing ball. The near-executioner was my old friend, Brooks Watson. Brooks is left-handed—which makes him lethal when you put him on a court with three right-handers. Not only does he swing from the port side, but he is fifty pounds overweight, meaning if he misses you on his first swing his momentum keeps him in motion and he just might clobber you the second time around. One bloody afternoon it cost me $65 to have twelve stitches put in my chin after he clobbered me with his brand new $125 racquet.

My mistake came in thinking southpaws are like the rest of us. They aren't. They not only write backwards, but their backhand is really their forehand. Ever since being decked by Brooks's racquet I've kept a wary eye on all left-handers, especially bankers and real estate agents who sign contracts. You never can tell where they will wind up hitting you.

Even more dangerous is the ambidextrous player, like Kent Busing. Kent never wore the little safety string which attaches the racquet to your wrist. Instead, he switched his racquet back and forth between hands—meaning he hit forehands from both sides of the court and never hit a backhand shot.

181

Once, in Nashville, Tennessee, I played with Al Jaynes. He uses a bent racquet, which is a cross between a hockey stick and one of those baskets used by Jai-Alai players to scoop the ball and throw it against the wall. Since Al's my age, he's lost his power. But since he was using a racquet shaped like a hollowed-out gourd, he could catch the ball, wait until I was looking to see where it had gone, then hit me with it in the back of the head. Nice guy!

Up until then I had been an R-ball fanatic, often carrying my racquet, shoes and shorts with me when I traveled out of town. Now I've slowed down, choosing my partners with care.

I sometimes play with my psychologist friend, Harvey Hester, who—if he is behind and I'm getting ready to serve—will interrupt the game by asking if I hate my mother.

I also play with Al Reed who wears trifocals, which makes him even more dangerous than Brooks Watson.

I used to play with Buddy Tipton, an Assembly of God pastor from nearby Vero Beach. But on the rare occasions when I beat him, he would remind me he used to ride with a motorcycle gang and didn't like losing. I had enough problems dodging racquets without having to worry about being hit with a bicycle chain if I won. I finally told him our friendship was too valuable to spoil it by playing racquetball.

But my opponents were not my big problem. I was. One day I realized I was getting angry on the court. It always happened when I was playing in a threesome—called "cutthroat." Here three men play, rotating serves, with the server competing against the other two. My anger would flash whenever I was ahead and my partner began missing shots, allowing the server to pile up points.

I never threw my racquet, cussed or even spoke harshly to the offending player whose stupidity, ineptness or crass inability to return a ball caused me to lose. But on several occasions, when my partner would miss an easy shot, I would feel my eyes dilate and a taste of burnt copper would appear in my mouth.

Even though it only lasted a few seconds, I knew I had stepped across a thin line that could cause serious problems if I didn't handle it.

I talked this over with Dr. Hester one afternoon as we sat cooling off after an outdoor match. He said a lot of people have a deep-seated anger. Most Christians try to hide it, but it will definitely show up under stress.

I've been thinking about that. For years I've suspected most shouting preachers have a lot of pent-up anger. Maybe racquetball players are the same, for I do a lot of shouting on the court—especially when I miss an easy ball.

Now I've discovered my mental attitude affects my ability to play. If I miss a shot and angrily call myself "Stupid," it lowers my self-esteem and leaves me open for defeat. However, if after a goof-up I say aloud, "Robert Schuller"—then repeat his name seven times very rapidly—I quickly develop what the bishop of the Crystal Cathedral calls the "Be Happy Attitude." My anger, having no place to roost, moves westward toward California.

Dealing with my anger has made a big difference in my game. Now I lose nearly all the time—but I don't seem to mind it as much.

TEN

Grow Old Along With Me
'Cause There's Lots More to Come

It's a frightening feeling to wake up one morning and realize you've become what you always dreaded—old.

Everybody I know wants to get older. But who wants to get *old*? Not me.

My mother says she doesn't want to get any older. But that's because she's ninety. She told me one day she was ready to die, but I doubt it. I mean, she still does an awful lot of things to keep on living.

I remember my dad telling us kids about an old man back in Indiana named Purcell who worked for my grandfather in the grain elevator. Working in a grain elevator in the heat of summer is enough to make any man want to die.

One afternoon—after a particularly hot, dusty, sweaty, fly-stinging day in the grain bins—the old fellow went into a nearby stable to pray to die. Grandpaw Buckingham was working in the feedlot outside and heard him calling out to God.

"Dear Jesus, come quickly. Come and get old Purcell. It's so hot, so miserable. I just can't take it any longer. Come and take me home, sweet Jesus."

Grandpaw took his shovel handle and thumped on the door. Loudly.

There was a long period of silence and finally a frightened voice from within said, "Who's there?"

"It's the angel of the Lord, Purcell," Grandpaw roared. "I've heard your prayer."

There was an even longer period of silence and finally a quivering voice answered. "Purcell ain't here right now, but I'll let him know you've been asking about him."

I think my mother's like that. She says she's ready—but life on earth still has a lot of attraction. I know it does for me.

Old age is not a disease. It is a marvelous condition 'most everyone I know is eager to catch. Unfortunately, it's not contagious and too many folks shuffle off before their time. But when you consider the alternative, old age is a pretty good deal.

There are a number of ways to keep from growing old:
- You might want to take up smoking.
- Or drugs.
- Drinking and driving are a sure formula.
- Overeating will do it, too.
- Or, if you really want to keep from growing old, have an affair. And if you really want to speed things up, have an affair with the wife of a psychopathic policeman who loves to sit at home loading and unloading his pistol.
- Worrying is a sure way to guarantee a short life. I once had a friend who worried so much about losing his hair that he had a heart attack and died. His worrying accomplished two things: He never did go bald—and he never had to be concerned about growing old.

Jackie keeps telling me there is a difference between old and older. The idea is to *grow* old, she says—for a long period of time. One eighty-year-old man said, "If I'd known I'd live this long, I'd have taken better care of myself."

I first became aware of the aging process in my mid-forties. Oh, I had been aware of it for years. But things like having to shave, getting your first driver's license and having your first child—those are things you look forward to, things that advance you toward your goal of being grown up. It's the things that happen to you *after* you've grown up that let you know the process never stops—that what began as a tingle in your loins gradually becomes a chill down your spine.

"Why don't you just admit you need glasses," Jackie said one evening as she looked over at me, sitting on the sofa with the newspaper at arm's length.

"They've changed the type," I argued. "They keep trying to cram more stuff on the page. I'll tell you, people will eventually stop trying to read the paper if they keep this up."

But it wasn't just the newspaper. It was the speedometer on my car, the phone book and eventually my sermon notes. When that happened I knew I needed help. Something unpleasant was happening to my eyes.

I made an appointment with my friend, Dr. Willie Malone in Elizabethton, Tennessee. Willie is not only an optometrist (eye doctor, that is), he is a faith preacher and the pastor of a church which believes in faith healing. I fully expected him to examine my eyes and then call for the elders to anoint me with oil.

I knew I was in trouble the minute I walked into his office. He was wearing glasses. It was the same sensation you get when you show up for your weekly appointment with your marriage counselor only to be told by his receptionist to come back next week after his divorce is final.

"It's not your lack of faith," Willie smiled. "It's the fact you're growing old."

"Older," I corrected him. "Not old."

Ignoring my desperate attempts to hang on to that which had already disappeared, Willie went ahead to explain that after a person reaches what he called "that age," the muscles in the eyes begin to lose their elasticity. To help me along, he put me in (gasp!) bifocals.

My eye muscles aren't the only ones which don't stretch very well any more. I have similar problems with a number of my other muscles, including my memory muscle. It's most evident when it comes to remembering the names of people—like my grandchildren. At such times my mind resembles an ancient rubber band, hardened and corroded, ready to snap at the slightest exertion.

187

"My brain filled up in 1979," I tell people who wonder why I can't remember their names. "Anything I put into my brain after 1979 pushes something out the other side."

That's the reason most older folks decide to stop learning. They can't afford to. To learn something new after you're fifty means you have to forget something you learned before you're fifty—that is, unless you didn't fill your brain up as a child the way I did.

My biggest problem—other than trying to remember where I laid my glasses—is with people who grab my hand in some public place and say, "I'll bet you don't remember me, do you?"

I squint at them through my unstretchable eyes and usually say something stupid like "I may have forgotten your name, but I'd never forget a face like that."

I used to lie and say, "Sure, I remember you."

But this is an age of honesty—and chutzpah. When I say that, people often respond, "Yeah? Then who am I?"

"You're George Burns," I answer.

"George Burns? He's ninety years old."

"Well, you look just like him."

Or I answer, "Sure, I know you. You're Calvin Klein."

"Who?"

"Calvin Klein. Your name is right there on the seat of your pants."

I keep hearing about folks who can memorize phone books. But I can't even look up a number and remember it long enough to dial the phone. I have to keep glancing back and forth from the dial to the phone book—and that's quite a feat when you've forgotten where you placed your glasses and have to hold the phone book at arm's length and dial at the same time.

My wife is my best defense. When we are together and I see some glad-hander approaching whose name I have forgotten, I quickly introduce my wife first. "Well, well, look who's here. Have you met my wife, Jackie?"

That forces the glad-hander to introduce himself—unless he's the kind of fellow who leers at you and says, "Bet you don't remember me, do you?"

At which time I say, "Of course. Jackie, this is Yves St. Laurent, one of the few men I know who wears his name on his necktie."

Recently I've found myself responding to the "betcha-don't-remember-me" people by saying, "I'm embarrassed, but because of my brain damage...."

That's about as close to the truth as I can come without saying, "Not only have I forgotten your name, but I have forgotten where I am. What city is this, anyway?"

I've had that problem, too. In fact, one afternoon I stepped off the airplane in Kansas City and for the life of me could not remember why I was there. I knew where I was. I knew I had flown in from Atlanta. But I had spent my entire flight time working on a magazine article. I knew I was in the KC airport, but the monitor screen in my brain drew a big blank when I tried to call up why. It's terribly embarrassing to phone your secretary long distance and say, "I'm here in Kansas City and I don't know why."

But nothing's as bad as thinking you know who someone is, only to discover later he's someone else.

I first noticed the problem while on vacation at our cabin in the North Carolina mountains. When I was a boy, roaming the mountains during the long summers I spent there with my family, I played with a red-headed, freckle-faced boy who lived right across the ridge. His name was Kenneth Summey. Fifty years have passed and I've not seen him since. I never even think about him. That is, until I get to the mountains in the summer. Then, every time I see a redheaded man I find myself rushing out of the cabin exclaiming, "Well, well, Kenneth Summey!"

One evening it happened in front of my entire family. Mr. Osteen, whose children used to come across the chigger trail and play with our children, knocked on the door one evening to tell his two little girls it was time to come home. I flicked on the porch light, saw him standing there and said loudly, "Well, if it isn't Kenneth Summey!"

Of course it wasn't. It was Herbert Osteen. But he was too shy to correct me. He just let me stand there talking to "good old Kenneth" until he spotted the children inside and motioned for them to follow him home. After he had gone I wondered why Kenneth would be coming after the Osteen kids.

My children thought I had fallen out of my tree. They all knew Mr. Osteen and had never even heard of Kenneth Summey, who belonged to my childhood, not theirs. Mr. Osteen later told my embarrassed children not to feel bad. A lot of strange people from Florida visit North Carolina in the summer.

The next week I was working on the stone wall along the driveway which goes down to the paved road when a car pulled up and stopped. The man at the wheel leaned over and called my name. I wiped sweat from my eyes and—before I could stop myself—exclaimed, "Well, well, Kenneth Summey!"

Of course it wasn't. It was Jim Ballard, pastor of the Baptist church in town. I cleared my throat, made some apology about the sun and sweat, and hoped he hadn't heard what I called him—knowing full well he had.

The following summer when I was at the cabin for a two-week stretch by myself to finish up a book, it happened again. I was feeding the ponies in the side pasture when I saw a redheaded man coming up the drive. There was no doubt about it. I hollered out, "Good old Kenneth!" But it wasn't, of course. It never is. It was Wade Thompson, another preacher who used to live on our property.

I don't know what's wrong with me. I wonder what would happen if the real Kenneth Summey were to show up. I'd probably grab his hand and call him Smith Wigglesworth or some other name I've heard but can't forget. I never met Smith Wigglesworth. In fact, I think he lived in South Africa fifty years ago. But how could anyone ever forget a name like Smith Wigglesworth? You only have to hear it once and you remember it the rest of your life. But Kenneth Summey? For the life of me I simply can't understand why I never think of Kenneth Summey until I see a redheaded man, and then I go out of control.

The older I grow the more I do that sort of thing. One Tuesday morning I was having breakfast with Bruce Morgan in a back booth at Sambo's. We were just finishing our conversation when I looked up and saw a short, stylish man approaching, holding his coffee cup.

I instantly recognized him as Andy Allison, a Scottish friend who attended our church.

"Andy," I beamed, pumping his hand. "It's good to see you. Meet Bruce Morgan."

"Delighted to meet a Scotsman," Bruce said.

Andy sat down and we chatted for a few moments. Then Bruce said,

"By the way, who was that other Scotsman who testified at the church last Sunday? I thought his name was Andy Allison."

I suddenly felt sick. Very sick. The man next to me was not Andy at all. He was Wayne Roberts, a quiet, humble fellow who brought his wife to the church services every week in a wheelchair—and far more Irish than Scottish. He was so pleased that I had asked him to sit next to us that he was willing to put up with my calling him by some-one else's name. Oh, what now?

In good military fashion, I created a diversion. First a coughing spell, then I turned over my water. We were all on our feet and it was time to go.

I grabbed Bruce's arm and tried to pull him away, but not until he got in a cheery "Good to see you, Andy. Nice to talk to a Scotsman."

Outside in the car, fighting back waves of nausea, I looked up and saw through the window Mr. Roberts sitting at the table with his coffee, waving at me.

The next morning at the elders' meeting I confessed to my peers. They encouraged me. I was growing old, they said. Not only my eye muscle, but my brain muscle was losing its elasticity. Besides, one of the elders said, he had talked to Mr. Roberts yesterday afternoon and this explained why he was now speaking with a Scottish brogue.

The other guys thought it was hilarious. They pounded on the table and laughed so hard they cried. I cried, too. Having your brain flick off like the screen on your word processor when the electricity dims is a terrifying thing.

So here I am, just barely at midlife, and my teeth are breaking off, my hair is falling out, my eyes are going bad, and my memory muscle is stretched out like the elastic tops of my old racquetball socks. But I'm not ready yet to say, "Take me home, sweet Jesus."

Cosmetics may hide the wrinkles, a toupee can cover a bald spot and contact lenses can fool the public. But the only defense against a poor memory is the truth.

Go ahead and say it, "Betcha-don't-remember-my-name, do you?"

I won't be offended by your brass, if you won't be offended by my brain.

"Now what was your name again?"